the too many tomatoes cookbook

Classic & Exotic Recipes
from around the World

the too many tomatoes cookbook

Classic & Exotic Recipes
from around the World

Brian Yarvin

The Countryman Press
Woodstock, Vermont

ISBN 978-0-88150-803-1

Library of Congress Cataloging-in-Publication Data are available.

Cover and interior photos by the author
Book design and composition by Michelle Farinella Design

Published by The Countryman Press, P.O. Box 748, Woodstock, Vermont 05091

Distributed by W. W. Norton & Company, Inc., 500 Fifth Avenue, New York, NY 10110

Manufactured in Malaysia

10 9 8 7 6 5 4 3 2 1

First and foremost, I have to offer my deepest gratitude to the farmers who grow the tomatoes I love so much. Bob Muth, Tom Culton, John Foster, and Hope Pezzulla all opened their farms to me. I also want to thank the nameless growers who produced the two hundred or so pounds of fresh tomatoes that my wife and I consumed during the production of this book. It was always a pleasure.

Besides my local produce vendor (which is too good a secret to share), I want to thank the folks at the Horst Farm Market and the Fair Food Farm Stand for taking the time to talk with me. As for my local tailgate markets in Highland Park and Westfield, New Jersey, I'm not sure if I should thank them for being there or apologize for being such a tough customer. I'm grateful in either case.

Several chefs opened their kitchens to me, as well. Sean Cavanaugh from the John J. Jeffries Restaurant in Lancaster, Pennsylvania, and Chris DeLuna and Charlie Restivo at Naples 45 in Manhattan share a passion for cooking and a commitment to hard work that left me astounded.

I also had the chance to pick the brains of several tomato experts. Jack Rabin from the New Jersey Agricultural Experiment Station set me on the right track when it came to finding reference books, and Andrew F. Smith, the author of several tomato books himself, answered my tomato questions with calmness and warmth.

This book wouldn't have been possible without at least a few trips to the library. That meant that I had to go to ones with significant tomato collections. Most notable was the Salem County Historical Society in the deep south of New Jersey. Harlan Buzby went out of his way for me there. I also visited the Conrad N. Hilton Library at the Culinary Institute of America on more than one occasion. I apologize to all the people I disturbed each time I packed up my stuff to go their wonderful café.

Finally, I'd like to thank my agent, Michael Bourret, at Dystel & Goderich; my copy-editor, Dale Evva Gelfand; and the entire crew at The Countryman Press. Your efforts on my behalf have been superhuman. You've all been great.

what this book isn't – an introduction of sorts 15
the raw ingredients; fresh, crushed, peeled, canned 16

1. basics 18

2. salads and cold dishes 28

contents

5. Rice and Pasta 116

6. Pizza and Baked Goods 132

what This Book Isn't: An Introduction of sorts

When people heard that I was writing a tomato book, they asked about my gardening skills or what my favorite heirloom varieties were and under their breath muttered, "Just what *is* an heirloom tomato, anyway?"

When those pleasantries were out of the way, the conversation started hinting about the real reasons for writing a book like this: memories of childhood when Grandma made a sauce or a soup that thrilled us, or the discovery that an otherwise alien cuisine has tomato sauce and is therefore "safe" to try. Tomatoes are one of those threads that run between cultures and somehow help link them. We can have an authentic, local tomato soup on four continents.

Tomatoes appear in Italian recipes that our grandparents made and in dishes from Sierra Leone that we've almost—but not quite—tried. You can find tomatoes at three-star dining palaces and in sandwiches served at makeshift roadside stands. By cooking tomato recipes from around the world, we see how cuisines relate to each other.

So head to the kitchen, grab some tomatoes, and join me for a journey.

The Raw Ingredients; Fresh, Crushed, Peeled, Canned

Some of these recipes call for very specific tomatoes: heirlooms for a salad or plums for *passata*. But much of the time, they just call for "chopped, fresh tomatoes." Not the most precise of instructions. So what do you do? Go to your favorite market, find the best-looking tomatoes you can, and use them. Yes, your use of another sort of tomato will make it taste a bit different than the original test dish, but you'll have better results with great raw materials.

Most recipes that don't use fresh call for "canned crushed tomato or *passata*." In this case, substituting a different canned product won't work so well. Stick with the instructions. The recipes list the products they were first cooked and tested with.

While you should at least make a batch of *passata* (page 20) during harvest time, most of us, no matter how self-sufficient, will have to buy canned tomatoes at some point. A few things are important to remember: Don't be swayed by fancy brands or labels, check the date on the package, and buy the freshest you can. I've found that this has more impact on quality than anything else. And make sure you don't pick up products that are preflavored. Some have basil, oregano, or just too much salt. Tomato should be about itself, not an herb or spice.

Most American supermarkets have a huge section devoted to canned tomatoes. Not as big as cereal, soda pop, or cookies, but still larger than you might expect. For decades I've watched people struggle to decide between dozens of almost identical-looking cans. While each type will yield different results, people often chose randomly, exasperated at the wide variety. I made my own decision long ago: crushed. It most resembled the products I'd used in Italy. (See "On Buying Canned Tomatoes in Italy," page 184.) This makes life much easier at shopping time and allows me to take advantage of sales and volume discounts without wondering if I'm buying the right kind of product.

For some reason, tomato products in reclosable packages are double or triple the price of plain cans. Get around this by buying large cans and refrigerating the leftovers in glass or plastic containers. I find it can be stored at least a couple of days without problems.

Whatever you do, don't make the mistake I made all too often: dumping the entire can into whatever recipe I was making—and invariably turning it into red glop. Yes, they only sell it in 28-ounce cans, but that doesn't mean you have to add 28 ounces every time.

1. The Basics

Tomato Purée Base (Passata di Pomodoro)

Even in the sunniest parts of Italy, tomatoes aren't in season for more than a few months each year. Yet tomato sauces and soups always show up.

There's no secret to this: With a bit of processing, tomatoes can be put by beautifully. Traditionally, tomatoes are canned, but these days most people I know who do this at home freeze them. And that's what we'll do here. You can't just take a fresh tomato and throw it in the freezer, though; a bit more has to be done.

Passata or *passato*? In Italy you'll hear both. Indeed, "Passato di Pomodoro" seems to agree with the lessons you learn in Italian 101, but in this book, you'll see *passata* because it's also what you'll see on the shelves of supermarkets and Italian specialty stores.

This is one of those products that shows up in every kitchen in Italy: the pulp of plum tomatoes in a thick, almost liquid, form. Over there, it's most often sold in recloseable glass or cardboard containers, making it easy to add just a splash when you need it and throw the rest back in the fridge. Here in North America, it's sold as "tomato purée" and almost always in huge cans.

This recipe calls for a hand-cranked food mill, so make sure you have one— with all the correct pieces—before you start.

 ## Tomato Purée (Passata)

Makes 12 cups

10 pounds very ripe plum
　　tomatoes, cut in quarters
2 cups water
1 teaspoon salt

1. In a pot large enough to hold all the tomatoes, heat the water over medium heat, and bring to a simmer.

2. Mix in the tomatoes, and cook for about 15 minutes or until they start to soften and break down. Reduce the heat to low, add the salt, and keep cooking for about 2 hours or until the volume of liquid has reduced by one-third. Remove the pot from the heat, and let it cool for at least 30 minutes.

3. Hold your food mill over a large, clean bowl. Make sure the whole thing is solid; if it's not, you'll have a real mess on your hands. Put a bit of the cooked tomato in the mill and start cranking. Soon the soft pulp (along with a few well-cooked pieces of skin) will start collecting in the bowl. This is the *passata*—that is; the stuff that's passed through the mill.

4. When you've run all the tomatoes through, it's time to put

them up. I prefer freezing in small quantities. Place 1 cup of *passata* in a heavy-duty freezer bag, press all the air out, zip it shut, and label it clearly with both the contents and the date you prepared it. Place the filled bags in the very back and bottom of your freezer where they'll keep for at least three months.

Variation: I find one-cup packs to be most convenient, but this is far from universal. Half-cup portions make sense for lots of people, and I've seen individual plastic ice cube trays used, too. If you do that, repack the cubes in a tightly sealed plastic bag after they're frozen solid.

Personally, I believe that certain chefs prefer using these because they can squeeze them in their hands as part of the cooking process. Indeed, when I've tried this, it was strangely gratifying—in a messy sort of way, of course.

Note that setup is important here. You'll need a pot of salted boiling water and another big bowl of ice water right nearby. You'll also need a big slotted spoon to transfer the tomatoes from the heat to the cold. I prefer those wire ones sold in Chinese markets, but any that drain easily will do.

 Frozen Whole Peeled Tomatoes (Pomodori Pelati)

Makes 16 cups

10 pounds ripe plum tomatoes
2 tablespoons salt for the
    boiling water

1. Cut an X across the bottom of each tomato; this will help get the peel off. Then put 6 of the tomatoes in boiling water, and cook them for 2 minutes, remove them with the slotted spoon, and put them straight into the ice water. After they're chilled for 2 minutes, you should be able to easily peel off the skins. Discard the skins, and save the interior pulp.

2. When you've blanched and peeled all the tomatoes, it's time to put them up for freezing. I find that 2-cup packages work best, but take a moment to decide how much you typically use *before* everything is packed up and becomes rock solid. Then put the tomatoes into well-marked plastic bags, press as much air as you can out of them, and pop them in the freezer. Try for the very back and bottom where it's coldest. Once they're frozen, they'll be ready for anything you can come up with.

This doesn't seem to be a traditional method, but it produces intense flavor and great texture. Use this in any recipe that calls for *passata* for a deeply flavored variation.

🌿 Roasted Puréed Tomatoes

Makes 9 cups

10 pounds ripe plum tomatoes,
    cut in half lengthwise
1 tablespoon salt
1 teaspoon freshly ground
    black pepper
Olive oil or cooking oil spray
    for the baking sheet

1. Preheat your oven to 325 degrees.

2. Arrange the tomato pieces on an oiled baking sheet, and bake for about 90 minutes or until the tomatoes have broken down and begin to brown. Remove them from the oven and let cool.

2. Put the cooled tomato pieces in a food processor, and purée until there are no more large lumps. Pack and freeze using the instructions for *passata* on page 20.

OK . . . I wanted to offer a recipe for sun-dried tomatoes, but I couldn't figure out a way to promise you sunshine. An oven should be a bit easier.

Sun-dried tomatoes are called for in many recipes, but you don't really need one. A sandwich of them with olive oil, salt, and pepper—or even just a fistful—is enough.

Oven-Dried Tomatoes

Makes 6 cups

5 pounds plum or cherry
    tomatoes, cut in half
    lengthwise
1/4 cup fine sea salt

1. Preheat your oven to 225 degrees.

2. Spread the tomatoes out on a baking sheet with the cut side facing upward and none touching each other. Sprinkle with the salt.

3. Bake for 3 hours or until the tomatoes start to look like they're cooking. Reduce the temperature to 175 degrees, and keep baking for about 6 more hours or until the tomatoes are shriveled up and almost leathery. (Bear in mind: Small tomatoes will dry MUCH faster than larger ones.) I use a commercial sun-dried tomato as a guide for doneness.

4. When they're done, let them cool, and store them in an airtight jar or plastic bag.

The Tomato and Other Poisons

Sometimes I think that New Jersey has more myths and legends about it than any other place. From the Jersey Devil to the Sopranos, we've heard it all. Yet we seem to believe the tale of the guy who ate a tomato on the steps of some courthouse to prove it wasn't poison.

You know it: A man named Robert Gibbon Johnson stood on the steps of the Salem County Courthouse and ate a tomato in front of a large crowd. We're told that everyone thought the tomato was poison, and he was going to prove them wrong. Indeed, some tellers of this tale even give a date for the event: September 1820. I've even seen a photo of a historical reenactment—one costumed actor chomping down on a whole beefsteak while another stands, mouth agape. Descriptions often mention large, excited crowds who were disappointed to see Johnson survive.

Although I don't remember the first time I heard it, I believed this story my entire adult life. That is, until I started poking around in New Jersey's vast tomato growing/cooking/studying subculture. It didn't take much digging to learn that not only is there no proof that this event ever happened, serious tomato historians even identified the person who made the whole thing up.

In 1820, Salem was a buzzing agricultural town on Delaware Bay and certainly home to a sailor or two. Those sailors would certainly have noticed that tomatoes were grown and eaten in both Europe and Latin America and were even quite popular in Louisiana (then a brand-new addition to the United States, thanks to a recent purchase). Our man Johnson owned a cookbook from 1812 that had a tomato recipe or two in it, and just a little bit more recently, in 1835, tomatoes were said to be a major crop in Salem county.

It just couldn't be that one guy didn't die and then fifteen years later, everybody was eating them.

Southern New Jersey was once a major tomato source. Farmers, often Italian immigrants, brought seeds from the old country and grew a legendary product. Campbell's built a big soup plant in Camden, and Salem was the home to a large ketchup factory and thirty smaller canneries. This legacy was celebrated with millions of bowls of tomato soup and more millions of plates of spaghetti and sauce.

Those plants are long gone, but tomato farming still lives—not for industrial processing, but for the chic markets of New York and Philadelphia. There, a single heirloom tomato sells for three or four dollars—enough to buy a gallon of canned tomato soup or heaven knows how much ketchup.

Poison? No. Stuff of legend? Well . . .

2. salads and cold dishes

Tomatoes were brought to Africa during the Colonial era, and today they show up in all sorts of dishes. This salad is pretty basic—but also pretty unique.

❧ African Tomato Salad
Makes 4 servings

3 cups chopped fresh tomatoes

2 tablespoons minced fresh
    hot chili pepper

1/2 cup chopped scallions

1 teaspoon salt

1 teaspoon sugar

1/4 cup white vinegar

Toss the tomatoes, chili, scallions, salt, sugar, and vinegar together and let stand for at least 20 minutes before serving.

Albanian? Why not? This simple recipe is another in the genre of refrigerator pickles—a technique that's a great way to add flavor and make stuff last just a bit longer. Serve these chilled as part of a salad.

 ## Albanian-Style Marinated Green Tomatoes

Makes 4 cups

2 cups cider vinegar

3 tablespoons olive oil

2 tablespoons salt

2 teaspoons sugar

4 bay leaves

2 teaspoons freshly ground
   black pepper

2 cinnamon sticks

6 cloves

1 cup water

2 pounds green plum tomatoes

1. Combine the vinegar, oil, salt, sugar, bay leaves, pepper, cinnamon, and cloves with the water in a heavy pot, and bring to a boil. After boiling for 1 minute, reduce the heat to a simmer and let cook for 5 minutes or until the flavors have combined. Remove from the heat and cool to room temperature. If you proceed to the next step while the liquid is still hot, you'll cook the tomatoes instead of pickling them.

2. Wash the tomatoes, pat them dry, and place them in a sealable, nonmetallic container. Pour the vinegar and spice liquid over them and rap the container on the counter a few times to get rid of bubbles. Cover and refrigerate.

3. Give the container a couple of shakes once or twice a day, but leave it in the fridge. The tomatoes are ready to eat after three days and will keep for several more weeks.

I've been thinking this one over and have decided that I will allow you to prepare this dish even if you can't pronounce it correctly; you just have to give the Italian way a try.

"Bru-sket-ta," Never "bru-shet-ta." Never, ever, ever.

Now that we've got pronunciation out of the way, we can make this classic snack from Tuscany.

 ## Bruschetta with Tomato

Makes 8 bruschette

2 cups chopped fresh tomatoes

1/4 cup chopped fresh
   basil leaves

1/4 cup plus 3 tablespoons
   extra-virgin olive oil

2 tablespoons red wine vinegar

1/2 teaspoon salt

1 long loaf Italian bread,
   cut into diagonal slices

2 cloves garlic, cut in half

1. Preheat your oven to 400 degrees.

2. Combine the tomatoes, basil leaves, 3 tablespoons of the olive oil, vinegar, and salt in a bowl and toss. Make sure everything is well mixed.

2. Take a slice of the bread, rub it with a piece of garlic, and brush it with some of the remaining 1/4 cup of oil. Repeat with the rest of the slices, and then lay the slices out on a cookie sheet, oil side up.

3. Bake for about 8 minutes, or until the tops of the bread begin to toast. Remove from the oven and spread a dollop of the tomato mixture on each slice of bread. They should all be fully covered. Return to the oven for 4 more minutes to warm the tomato and finish the toasting process. Serve immediately.

Everyone who's been in an American diner knows what Greek salad is, right? That big bowl of lettuce (usually iceberg) with some feta cheese, canned stuffed grape leaves (if you're lucky), and a couple of anchovy fillets on top. Is that what they eat in Greece? I was dubious. I don't recall Greek cuisine ever being big on lettuce; instead, this is what I found. . . .

 ## Greek Salad (Horiatiki)
Makes 4 servings

1/4 cup extra-virgin
   olive oil
3 tablespoons lemon juice
5 anchovy fillets, chopped
2 tablespoons capers,
   rinsed and drained
1 teaspoon dried oregano
1/2 teaspoon dried mint
1/4 teaspoon salt

1/2 teaspoon freshly
   ground black pepper
2 cups coarsely chopped
   ripe tomatoes
1 cup chopped cucumber
1 cup chopped bell pepper
1/2 cup chopped red onion
1 cup crumbled feta cheese
1 cup Greek olives

1. Combine the olive oil, lemon juice, anchovies, capers, oregano, mint, salt, and pepper in a closeable plastic or glass container, and mix well. Let stand at least 30 minutes so the flavors can combine.

2. Mix the tomatoes, cucumber, bell pepper, onion, feta, and olives in a large bowl, and pour the olive oil mixture over it. Toss and serve immediately.

Note: If you're making this salad ahead of time, prepare the dressing and chop the vegetables, but don't combine them until you're ready to take them to the table.

Not long ago I thought that salmon was a cold-water fish that would never make it to the tropical shores of Hawaii. How wrong I was.

 ## Hawaiian-Style Salmon Salad (Lomi Lomi Salmon)

Makes 4 servings

8 ounces salt-cured salmon
    (lox works fine here),
    cut into small pieces
1/2 cup chopped Maui onion
3 cups chopped fresh tomatoes
1 tablespoon finely chopped
    hot chili pepper
1 tablespoon fresh lime juice
1/2 teaspoon freshly ground
    white pepper
2 cups Bibb lettuce leaves,
    washed and drained

1. Toss the salmon, onion, tomatoes, chili pepper, lime juice, and ground pepper together in a large bowl. Set aside for 30 minutes to let the flavors combine.

2. Arrange the lettuce leaves on a serving plate and heap the salmon mixture on top.

3. Serve at room temperature to preserve the flavor of the tomatoes.

Is there a psychiatric diagnosis for "fear of heirloom tomatoes?" If there is, I've suffered from it. There have been so many times that I've blown ten or twelve bucks on the most beautiful heirloom tomatoes imaginable—and then watched them rot away because I couldn't bring myself to cut them up and eat them. Photograph them? Yes. Boast about them to my friends as if they were a new boat or sports car? Yes. Cut them up and eat them? No.

But some people do it—indeed, great chefs do it—and I'm going to do it, also.

 ## Heirloom Tomato Salad

Makes 4 servings

1. Mix the tomatoes, capers, oil, vinegar, salt, pepper, and basil leaves in a large, nonmetallic bowl, and mix well. Make sure the ingredients are evenly distributed.

2. Cover and let stand for 30 minutes before serving to allow the flavors to combine. Serve promptly.

3 cups chopped
   heirloom tomatoes*
1 tablespoon capers,
   rinsed and drained
2 tablespoons extra-
   virgin olive oil
1 tablespoon white
   wine or sherry
   vinegar
1/2 teaspoon sea salt
1/2 teaspoon freshly
   ground black
   pepper
2 or 3 fresh basil leaves
*Try to choose a mixture
 of smaller tomatoes in
 different sizes
 and colors.

Just What Is an Heirloom Tomato?

I had hoped that tomato farmers—as idealistic as they are—wouldn't be the sorts of people to get into feuds, but this simple question seems to be the one most likely to raise their blood pressure.

Today, most tomatoes that we encounter in supermarkets are hybrids. That is, they're crosses between several tomato varieties that may well have been selected for reasons other than taste. This makes them more likely to survive the trip to the supermarket but not quite as interesting when it's time to cook or eat them. Besides the flavor, there's another issue here: If you collect the seeds of a hybrid and replant them, they aren't likely to produce plants that are the same as their parents. So if you want to grow them again, you'll have to buy the seeds again next season. (Needless to say, this is great for seed companies.)

Open-pollinated tomatoes are a different story altogether. Save the seeds, plant them, and they grow up to have the same traits as the previous generation. Repeat this process for a while, and you have an heirloom—something that's been around for a long time.

So where's the conflict? It seems to boil down to a couple of questions: How long has a certain variety been around? And if it's an open-pollinated tomato that's only been grown for a few years, is it an heirloom? To add fuel to the feud, if it's a really popular hybrid that's been grown for decades, some people will describe it as an "heirloom" even though it doesn't meet the technical standards. If more than a few farmers/vendors/scholars/consumer groups could agree on these (and

other) matters, there'd be an official definition, but they don't, so there isn't.

At farm markets (and even supermarkets) around here, my fellow shoppers simply define heirloom tomatoes as "the ones that taste great and look cool." That definition might not be technically right, but it gets to the point.

Back in the early '80s when South American restaurants started popping up in New York, ceviche was still pretty much unknown. Its status as the highest-priced item on many menus didn't do much for its popularity, and the fact that it contained uncooked fish didn't help much, either. These days, though, ceviche has gone upscale and appears in all sorts of places.

 ## Marinated Seafood with Tomatoes (Ceviche)

Makes 4 servings

1/2 cup fresh lime juice

1/4 cup fresh lemon juice

1 tablespoon chopped
    fresh hot green pepper

1/4 cup chopped red onion

1/2 teaspoon salt

1 cup bay scallops

1 cup squid rings

1 cup peeled and deveined shrimp

1 cup chopped tomato

2 tablespoons chopped fresh coriander

1. Combine the lime juice, lemon juice, green pepper, red onion, and salt in a large nonmetallic bowl. Then add the scallops, squid rings, and shrimp. Mix well, making sure that the seafood is well coated with juice. Refrigerate for at least 8 hours or until the flesh of the shrimp becomes opaque. Be aware that after 24 hours the flesh will become rubbery and tough.

2. Add the tomato and coriander and mix well. Serve immediately.

Tabbouleh is the most well-known grain salad. It's made from bulgur, a slightly processed wheat product that many people confuse with its cousin couscous—but it's a whole different taste and texture.

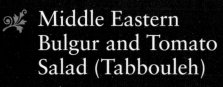

Middle Eastern Bulgur and Tomato Salad (Tabbouleh)

Makes 4 servings

1 cup bulgur

2 1/2 cups water

2 cups chopped fresh tomatoes

1 teaspoon salt

1/4 cup lemon juice

1/4 cup extra-virgin olive oil

1/4 cup chopped red onion

1/2 cup chopped parsley

2 tablespoons chopped
fresh mint leaves

1/2 teaspoon freshly ground
black pepper

1. Put the bulgur in a large bowl with the water and let it soak for at least 2 hours or until tender. If any liquid remains at the end, drain it. Set the bulgur aside.

2. Toss the tomatoes and salt together so that they're well mixed. Place in a colander for about 1 hour so that the liquid can drain off.

3. Combine the bulgur, tomatoes, lemon juice, olive oil, onion, parsley, mint, and ground pepper, and mix well. Serve at room temperature; chilling will kill the tomato taste.

Variation: You can add finely chopped raw garlic and/or hot chili peppers to give the salad a little extra zing.

Like anything else on the Thai menu, salads have an intense blast of sweet, sour, hot, and salty flavors.

🌿 Thai Salad of Green Papaya and Cherry Tomatoes

Makes 4 servings

1 quart water

1 cup long beans, cut into 1-inch pieces*

2 Thai green chilies or bird peppers, chopped

2 cloves garlic, crushed and chopped

2 tablespoons crushed roasted peanuts**

1 tablespoon dried shrimp

1 tablespoon brown sugar

1/4 cup fresh-squeezed lime juice

3 tablespoons Thai fish sauce

1 cup halved cherry tomatoes

2 cups shredded green papaya

1 cup mung bean sprouts

*Substitute string beans if you don't like or can't find long ones.

**Crush the peanuts by first putting them in a sealable plastic bag and then hammering them with a mallet.

1. Bring the water to a boil, reduce the heat to a simmer, add the long beans, and cook for about 20 minutes or until they're tender. Drain and set aside.

2. Combine the chilies, garlic, peanuts, shrimp, sugar, lime juice, and fish sauce in a nonmetallic container and let stand for at least 1 hour.

3. Put the cooked beans, tomatoes, papaya, and sprouts in a bowl, and toss with the dressing. Serve immediately.

Note: You can make the dressing ahead, but you must combine it with the beans, tomatoes, papaya, and sprouts at the last second. If you let it stand, the whole thing will turn to mush.

All sorts of recipes were created to hide the flaws of less-than-perfect ingredients, but few exist to show off the best of what you've got. *Insalata Caprese* is one of those. Make it when you've got beautiful tomatoes and great, fresh mozzarella. Anything less will be a disappointment.

❧ Tomato and Mozzarella Salad (Insalata Caprese)
Makes 4 servings

2 cups sliced fresh tomatoes

2 cups fresh mozzarella cheese, drained and sliced thin

1/4 cup loosely packed fresh basil leaves, rinsed and drained

3 tablespoons extra-virgin olive oil

3 tablespoons red wine vinegar

1/2 teaspoon salt

1/2 teaspoon freshly ground black pepper

1. Alternately lay the slices of tomato and mozzarella on a large serving plate. When finished, a thin layer of tomato and cheese should cover the plate.

2. Place the basil leaves over the cheese and tomato. Then pour (I hate the word "drizzle" in this context) the oil and vinegar over the plate, sprinkle with the salt and pepper, and serve immediately at room temperature.

Note: Nothing will ruin one of these salads more completely than a stay in the fridge. The cold hurts the flavor of the tomatoes and congeals the mozzarella.

Not long ago, chilled gelatin salads were considered perfect at a summer lunch. Today though, they seem archaic. But having both vegetables and protein—not to mention a fun, squiggly texture—aspics are ready for a comeback.

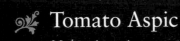

🌿 Tomato Aspic

Makes 4 servings

4 cups tomato juice, divided

2 packets gelatin crystals

1 cup chopped cucumber

1/2 cup shredded carrot

1/2 cup chopped yellow
   bell pepper

1/4 cup chopped scallions

1/2 teaspoon hot sauce

1 tablespoon Worcestershire
   sauce

1. Warm 2 cups of the tomato juice in a saucepan over medium heat. When it begins to bubble a bit, remove it from the heat and transfer to a Pyrex or ceramic dish large enough to hold all the ingredients.

2. Sprinkle the gelatin crystals onto the warm tomato juice and stir until dissolved—this may take a bit of work. Make sure there's none caked up on the bottom.

3. Mix in the remaining 2 cups of tomato juice, the cucumber, carrot, bell pepper, scallions, hot sauce, and Worcestershire and refrigerate. The aspic is ready to serve when it's completely solidified, about 4 hours.

There's got to be something you can put in a bowl of salad besides lettuce, tomato, cucumber, and maybe some sprouts. How about a can of beans? It makes all the difference in the world.

❧ Turkish White Bean Salad (Fasulye Piyazi)

Makes 4 servings

1 can (15.5 ounces) white beans,
   rinsed and drained
2 cups chopped fresh tomatoes
1/2 cup chopped onion
1/4 cup chopped scallion greens
1/4 cup chopped parsley
1/4 cup extra-virgin olive oil
3 tablespoons freshly squeezed
   lemon juice
1/2 teaspoon salt
1/4 teaspoon freshly ground
   black pepper

1. In a large bowl, combine the beans, tomatoes, onion, scallion, and parsley. Make sure everything is well mixed. If you're making the dish ahead of time, set it aside. Proceed to step 2 just before serving.

2. Add the olive oil, lemon juice, salt, and pepper, and toss, making sure that the oil and juice coat the entire salad. Serve immediately.

Was this dish created as a way to use leftover bread, overripe tomatoes, or maybe even surplus basil? There are tales that claim these things. I'd like to see it appreciated for another reason though: It tastes really good.

Tuscan Bread-and-Tomato Salad (Panzanella)

Makes 4 servings

2 cups stale French or Italian
   bread cut into 1-inch cubes
2 cups chopped fresh tomatoes
1/2 cup chopped red onion
1/2 cup chopped yellow
   bell pepper
1/4 cup chopped Italian parsley
1/4 cup red wine vinegar
1/2 cup extra-virgin olive oil
1 teaspoon salt
1/2 teaspoon freshly ground
   black pepper

Combine the bread, tomatoes, onion, bell pepper, parsley, vinegar, olive oil, salt, and ground pepper in a large bowl, making sure all the ingredients are evenly distributed. Let stand for at least 2 hours. It's ready when the bread has absorbed all the liquid. Serve cold.

The Chefs: Sean Cavanaugh, Is This Pennsylvania Dutch?

If you've visited Amish communities, you'll quickly get a sense of the local restaurant food: roast meats, thick sauces, sweet and sour sides, and even sweeter desserts. Spend a few more hours exploring, and a paradox emerges: Roadside stands sell the most exquisite produce you'll ever see, and restaurants somehow seem to be the only ones who don't notice.

Enter Sean Cavanaugh, chef/owner of the John J. Jefferies Restaurant in downtown Lancaster, Pennsylvania, center of the most well-known Amish settlement in the country. Sean wanted to cook with those ingredients. He told me he searched the whole country for the best resources possible and wound up here—right down the road from those thousand seat buffets.

Don't get me wrong, Sean has a healthy respect for what the Amish themselves eat. He said, "How they cook, it's been bastardized, the farmers are still cooking hearts and liver and kidneys; they have good appetites because they're active. They don't eat this processed food." He tries to do the same and incorporate every part of the animal in a locally based fine cuisine. There's tripe in his soups, liver in his patés, and at the height of harvest season, tomatoes with everything.

Even the names of Sean's dishes speak of his passion; he calls his heirloom salad "Farmer Tom's Tricked-Out Heirloom Tomatoes." His raw beef with tomatoes dish is called "The Truth"—the menu asks, "Can you handle the truth?" And he makes a sadly tomatoless pork-liver dish called "Joe's Love Squared." If all that doesn't convince you, the menu urges you to "Please say no to factory farms and start thinking about where your food comes from. . . ."

Is this the future? I'm no expert and can't predict. Maybe we should ask, "Is this the future for small farms squeezed into urbanizing areas?" and "Is this a better way to market the Amish passion for farming than jars of jam and foam trays of cookies?"

Day and weekend trips to Lancaster County are a tradition for families from all over the Northeast. A meal in a place like John J. Jefferies and some produce from Tom Culton (page 200) and the Horst Farm Market (page 96) might well be what's needed to put this place on the gastronomic map.

BTW, if the chef is named Sean Cavanaugh, who's John J. Jefferies? A big investor? A famous farmer? No . . . his was the name on an inspection document from the 1890s found while renovating the building.

3. soups

"White tomato?" Is this a rare heirloom? No. It's just a reference to the way it's made. This simmered and strained meat-and-tomato broth is almost like a stock.

For a quick hearty soup, you can add fresh or frozen vegetables and/or leftover meats.

Hungarian White Tomato Broth (Feher Paradicsomleves)

Makes 4 servings

6 cups chicken broth
3 cups canned whole tomatoes
1 teaspoon salt

1. Heat the broth and tomatoes in a saucepan over medium-low heat. Crush the tomatoes a bit with a couple of strokes from a potato masher. Cook uncovered, occasionally stirring, for about 60 minutes or until about one-quarter of the liquid has evaporated.

2. Strain out the solid pieces of tomato and reserve the remaining broth. If you're making this soup ahead of time, set it aside in the fridge.

3. When ready to serve, return the broth to the pot and taste it. Add the salt if needed. Serve warm.

In this part of the world, soups are meals, and this dish should be thought of as the centerpiece of a South American lunch or dinner. Serve with rice and beans on the side.

🌿 Ecuadorian Fish, Yucca, and Plantain Soup (Sancocho de Pescado)

Makes 4 servings

1/2 cup lemon juice

1/2 teaspoon salt

1/2 teaspoon freshly
   ground white pepper

1 pound white-fleshed
   fish fillets, cut into
   1-inch pieces*

4 cups fish broth

2 cups green plantain
   chunks

1 cup peeled and
   chopped yucca**

1 ear of corn, sliced into
   1-inch sections

2 tablespoons peanut oil

1/2 teaspoon dried thyme

1 teaspoon annatto paste

1 cup chopped onion

1 cup chopped green
   bell pepper

2 cups chopped fresh
   tomatoes

*When it doubt, use tilapia.
It's the easiest to find.

**Use frozen if need be.

1. Mix the lemon juice, salt, and white pepper together in a nonmetallic bowl, and add the fish. Let it marinate in the refrigerator for at least 1 hour. If it looks like it's drying out, spoon some more juice on it.

2. Bring the broth to a boil in large saucepan, and add the plantain, yucca, and corn. Lower the heat to medium, and simmer covered, stirring occasionally, for about 20 minutes or until the yucca is fork tender. Set aside.

3. Heat the oil, thyme, annatto, onion, pepper, and tomatoes in a skillet over medium heat, and cook, stirring, until the onion is translucent. Add the fish, and continue cooking for about 20 minutes or until the fish is cooked through.

4. Stir the fish mixture into the pot of broth. Simmer over medium-low heat for about 15 minutes or until the corn is tender. Serve hot.

Not every Indian dish has a long list of ingredients. This soup is a really easy way to get those flavors on the table without resorting to mixes or powders.

Indian-Style Ginger and Tomato Soup

Makes 4 servings

1 tablespoon chopped fresh
   hot green pepper
2 tablespoons chopped
   fresh ginger
1 teaspoon sugar
6 cups chopped fresh tomatoes
1 tablespoon butter

1. Put the hot pepper, ginger, sugar, and tomatoes in a pot over medium-low heat, and cook, stirring occasionally, for about 40 minutes or until the tomatoes have broken down and the pepper is tender.

2. Remove the tomato mixture from the heat and purée with an immersion blender or food processor.

3. Return the purée to the pot. Heat over medium heat and mix in the butter. Simmer for 5 more minutes. Serve immediately.

Soups are the unsung heroes of Indian cuisine. While curries get all the glory, soups sit quietly in the background, just waiting for us to give them a try.

Indian Tomato and Lentil Soup (Rasam)

Makes 4 servings

1 cup yellow lentils

4 cups plus 1 cup water

1 tablespoon peanut oil

1 teaspoon mustard seed

1 teaspoon ground coriander

1 teaspoon ground cumin

1 teaspoon freshly ground black pepper

1 cup chopped onion

3 cloves garlic, chopped

1 teaspoon curry leaves

1 teaspoon sugar

3 cups canned crushed
  tomatoes or *passata* (page 20)

1 tablespoon tamarind paste
  or concentrate

1. Put the lentils in a saucepan with 4 cups of the water and simmer covered for 90 minutes or until the lentils are tender. Drain and set aside.

2. Put the oil, mustard seed, coriander, cumin, and pepper in a large pan, and cook, stirring, until the oil begins to splatter and the spices release their fragrance, about 1 minute.

3. Lower the heat to medium-low, add the onions and garlic, and cook, occasionally stirring, until the onions start to turn golden, about 20 minutes.

4. Mix in the curry leaves, sugar, crushed tomatoes, tamarind paste, cooked lentils, and the remaining 1 cup of water. Simmer until the lentils are very tender, about 45 minutes. Serve warm.

When the weather turns cold, nothing is more soothing than a pot of soup like this one cooking on the stove.

Italian-Style Tomato Soup

Makes 4 servings

2 tablespoons olive oil

1 teaspoon dried oregano

2 cloves garlic, crushed

1/2 cup chopped onion

1/2 cup chopped celery

1/2 cup chopped carrot

1/2 cup chopped potato

2 cups canned crushed tomatoes or *passata* (page 20)

3 cups chicken, beef, or vegetable broth

1 tablespoon red wine vinegar

1 teaspoon sugar

1/2 teaspoon salt

1/2 teaspoon freshly ground black pepper

Grated Parmesan cheese for garnish

1. Heat the oil, oregano, and garlic in a heavy pot over medium heat, and cook, stirring, until the garlic begins to brown at the edges, about 10 minutes.

2. Add the onion, celery, carrot, and potato, cooking until the potato and onion begin to brown and the carrot is softening, about 30 minutes.

3. Mix in the tomatoes, broth, vinegar, sugar, salt, and pepper, and simmer uncovered for about 30 minutes or until roughly one-quarter of the liquid has evaporated and the vegetables are completely tender. Serve hot topped with grated Parmesan.

What?! Mexican food other than tacos and enchiladas?!

Mexican-Style Meatball Soup (Albondigas)

Makes 4 main-course servings

1 tablespoon peanut oil

1/2 teaspoon ground chili powder

1 cup chopped onion

2 cups canned crushed tomatoes
    or *passata* (page 20)

1 quart chicken broth

8 ounces ground beef

8 ounces ground pork

2 cloves garlic, crushed and chopped

1 teaspoon dried oregano

1 teaspoon salt

1/2 teaspoon freshly ground
    black pepper

1 egg

1/4 cup chopped fresh cilantro

1. Heat the oil, chili powder, and onion in a large saucepan over medium heat. Cook, stirring, until the onion has turned translucent.

2. Mix in the crushed tomatoes and chicken broth. Reduce the heat to medium-low, and simmer covered, occasionally stirring, for about 20 minutes or until the broth and tomatoes have melded into a soup.

3. Combine the beef, pork, garlic, oregano, salt, pepper, egg, and cilantro in a large bowl and mix—your hand works great here—until all the ingredients are evenly distributed.

4. Form the meat mixture into golf ball–size spheres and add to the simmering soup. Cook, occasionally stirring, for about 40 minutes or until the meatballs are cooked all the way through. (You might have to cut open a meatball to check.) Serve warm.

So how do you tell an authentic Mexican restaurant from one meant for gringos? Easy! Look for this dish on the menu. Nothing will chase dilettantes away like a big bowl of well-seasoned tripe. Of course, this brings up the all-important subject of the tripe itself. Mexican cooks use honeycomb tripe, which is the easiest to find and the hardest to cook. Those with access to a good butcher (especially in an Asian store) can find bible tripe or omasum. Bible tripe can be cooked in about an hour (instead of the 4 hours needed for honeycomb) and gives a very similar rich and gamey flavor. And tripe, any kind of tripe, can't be called "gringo."

Mexican Tripe Soup (Menudo)

Makes 6 servings

1 tablespoon peanut oil

2 Mexican chorizo sausages, chopped

1/2 teaspoon dried thyme

1 teaspoon dried oregano

1 teaspoon ground cumin

1/2 teaspoon freshly ground black pepper

2 cloves garlic, crushed and chopped

1 cup chopped onion

1 cup canned crushed tomatoes or *passata* (page 20)

1 can (15 ounces) white hominy, rinsed and drained

1 pound bible tripe or omasum, cut into 1-inch strips

1/4 cup chopped fresh cilantro

4 cups beef broth

1/2 teaspoon salt

1. Heat the oil and chorizo sausage in a Dutch oven on medium heat, and cook, stirring, for about 5 minutes or until the meat begins to brown and fat renders out and into the pot.

2. Add the thyme, oregano, cumin, pepper, garlic, and onion, and cook, stirring, until the onion becomes translucent, about 20 minutes.

3. Mix in the tomatoes, hominy, tripe, cilantro, and broth. Bring the mixture to a boil for 1 minute. Reduce the heat to medium-low, and simmer uncovered, occasionally stirring, for about 1 hour or until the tripe is thoroughly cooked and tender.

4. Just prior to serving, taste the broth, and add the salt if needed. Serve hot.

What is this stuff called "quinoa?"

Well, it's a seed that's kind of like a grain, and it's a nice change from rice and beans.

How do you pronounce it?

People around here say "keen-wah."

And why should it be in a soup?

It tastes pretty good when you cook it with liquid and seasonings.

Are you ready?

Quinoa and Tomato Soup
Makes 4 servings

1/2 cup quinoa, rinsed
   and drained

1 cup water

1 tablespoon olive oil

1 cup chopped onion

3 cloves garlic, crushed
   and chopped

3 cups canned
   tomato purée

1 teaspoon salt

1/2 teaspoon freshly
   ground black
   pepper

2 cups chicken broth*

*Use mushroom broth
to make this
dish vegan.

1. Combine the quinoa and water in a small saucepan, and bring to a boil over high heat. Reduce the heat to low, and simmer covered for 20 minutes or until all the liquid is absorbed. Remove from the heat and set aside.

2. Heat the oil, onion, and garlic in a large pot over medium heat, and sauté for about 20 minutes or until the onion is translucent and the garlic begins to brown at the edges. Add the tomato purée, salt, pepper, and broth, and cook, occasionally stirring, for about 15 minutes or until the flavors combine.

3. To serve, mound some cooked quinoa at the bottom of a bowl and then ladle the hot tomato soup over it.

Is American the most exotic cuisine? Maybe not—but gumbo is one of our most exotic dishes. Hailing from the bayous of Louisiana and known as a cornerstone of Cajun cooking, it's the subject of songs, folk tales, and even recipes. This one, with two bayou favorites—shrimp and crab—is pretty classic.

Shrimp and Crab Gumbo

Makes 6 servings

3 tablespoons peanut oil

3 tablespoons all-purpose flour

1/2 teaspoon paprika

1/2 teaspoon crushed red pepper

1/2 teaspoon dried thyme

1/2 teaspoon dried oregano

1 bay leaf

1 cup chopped onion

4 cloves garlic, crushed and chopped

1 cup chopped green bell pepper

1/2 cup chopped celery

2 cups chopped fresh tomatoes

2 cups sliced okra

4 cups fish stock or broth

1/2 teaspoon freshly ground black pepper

8 ounces peeled raw shrimp

8 ounces fresh crabmeat

1 teaspoon salt

4 cups cooked white rice

1. Combine the oil and flour in a large pot over medium heat. Stir continuously until a thick paste forms and it turns golden, about 3 minutes. This is the roux base.

2. Mix in the paprika, red pepper, thyme, oregano, and bay leaf. Make sure they're coated with the roux.

3. Reduce the heat to medium-low, add the onion, garlic, bell pepper, and celery. Cook, stirring, until the onion is translucent and the bell pepper is tender, about 15 minutes.

4. Add the tomatoes and okra, cooking until the okra is tender and the tomatoes start to break down, about 20 minutes.

5. Mix in the fish stock and ground pepper, raise the heat, and bring the mixture to a boil for 1 minute. Reduce the heat to low, and let the mixture barely simmer uncovered until the vegetables have begun to break down into a soup, about 30 minutes. Though the heat is low, stir the gumbo occasionally to make sure it doesn't scorch.

6. Add the shrimp and cook until the shrimp turns opaque, about 10 minutes. Then mix in the crabmeat and give it a few more stirs to warm it through. Taste the soup, and add the salt only if necessary.

7. To serve, mound some rice at the bottom of a soup bowl, and ladle the warm soup over the rice.

The Tomato Growers: The Muth Family Farm

To find Bob Muth's farm, you'll have to travel to a part of the Garden State that most people don't think about. There are no major highways, no chemical plants, and no sports stadiums. Even so, the place is teeming with subdivisions and big-box stores; the Muth Family Farm is the last one left for quite a ways around. That's just one of the reasons no sign marks the farm entrance; as the lone survivor, people notice he's there.

When I started searching for the ultimate New Jersey tomato farmer, Bob's name came up again and again as the expert, the guru, the man to see. One of six children born on a farm near Glassboro, he had New Jersey soil in his veins. After college and grad school, he did a stint as a county agriculture agent in South Carolina but came back home when he saw the chance to work the family farm.

From the beginning his goal was to make the farm sustainable—that is, to reduce pesticide use to bare minimums and nurture the soil. He then began taking the fields organic—a process that required a minimum of three years with no chemicals. Thanks to those efforts, Bob is a member of that small club of New Jersey farmers who've expanded during the past decade. Today, he has a total of 118 acres, some organic and the rest moving in that direction.

The New Jersey tomato's legendary status was built on products that were canned. Fifty years ago, every agricultural town of any size had a packing plant, and tomato soup and ketchup were the most popular exports. This business left long ago, and taking its place is an entirely different tomato industry—and even an entirely different tomato. Today you'll find heirloom varieties grown organically, sizes that range from grape to softball, flavors from tart to sweet, and more colors than you knew a tomato could come in.

On breezy day in early May, Bob and I walked among the seedlings and attempted conversation. Me about tomatoes, he about soil. Out in the fields, he was so excited he could barely control himself, offering me handfuls of rich soil and explaining how he used a green plant called "vetch" as a cover crop to nourish it.

He then took me into the greenhouses, where baby tomato plants were being put in the ground. He showed me rows of his personal favorites: "Pineapple," "Cherokee Purple," and "Green Zebra." When I told him that Green Zebras were a favorite of mine, too, he countered by saying that on the farm, they call them "California Yuppie Tomatoes" because of the high price they commanded at a San Francisco farmer's market.

Bob then went on to say, "Heirloom tomatoes are like people: They may look funny, but they're damn good on the inside." Since the conversation was turning upbeat, I decided to ask him about what was coming next. "I wish I were twenty years younger!" he told me. "The markets are expanding, and the community is really interested in what I'm doing. The future is fan-*tastic*!"

Although he wanted to tell me more, he had to head back to the fields.

Is this like the stuff that comes in a can? I hope not! But it's a good, wholesome soup that has tomatoes as its main ingredient.

 ## Tomato Soup

Makes 4 servings

1 tablespoon butter

1/2 teaspoon dried thyme

1/2 teaspoon dried oregano

1/2 cup chopped onion

1 clove garlic, crushed and
   chopped

3 cups canned crushed
   tomatoes or *passata*
   (page 20)

3 cups chicken or vegetable
   broth

1/2 teaspoon salt

1/2 teaspoon freshly ground
   black pepper

1. Heat the butter, thyme, and oregano in a pot over medium heat, and cook, stirring, until the butter is melted and the herbs are well coated.

2. Lower the heat slightly, add the onion and garlic, and cook, stirring frequently, until the onion is translucent and beginning to brown at the edges, about 20 minutes.

3. Add the tomatoes, broth, salt, and pepper. Raise the heat to high, and bring the mixture to a boil for 1 minute. Then lower the heat to a simmer—you'll have to fuss with the heat a bit to make sure nothing scorches—and cook uncovered, stirring occasionally, until the mixture has reduced by about one-quarter. Serve warm.

Variation: If you want your soup as smooth as that canned one, let it cool, purée it in a blender, and reheat it before serving.

Who would believe it—a dish that uses tortilla chips as an ingredient! We're so used to thinking of them as a snack that we forget they're real food.

- -

Tortilla Soup (Sopa de Tortilla)

Makes 4 servings

1 tablespoon peanut oil

1 teaspoon dried oregano

1 teaspoon ground cumin

1/2 cup chopped onion

2 canned chipotle peppers, chopped

3 cloves garlic, crushed and chopped

1 cup chopped fresh tomatillo

1 cup chopped fresh poblano peppers

1 cup chopped fresh tomatoes

4 cups chicken broth

1/2 teaspoon salt

3 cups unflavored tortilla chips

1. Heat the oil, oregano, cumin, onion, chipotle, and garlic in a saucepan over medium heat, and cook, stirring frequently, until the onion begins to brown at the edges, about 15 minutes.

2. Mix in the tomatillo, poblano, and tomatoes, and continue to cook, occasionally stirring, until the bell pepper is tender, about 10 minutes.

3. Add the broth, and simmer until all the flavors combine, about 20 minutes. Taste and add the salt if needed.

4. Place a layer of tortilla chips at the bottom of the individual bowls. Ladle the finished soup over the chips and serve immediately.

Gazpacho: The Salad You Drink

I've always been surprised by the number of people who won't eat gazpacho ingredients chopped up in a bowl but will cheerfully down glass after glass of the same stuff puréed into a liquid. Purists will always ask if there's an "authentic" gazpacho, and we'll have that recipe, but there are others, including a Southwestern-style gazpacho for chili fanatics and, for all those people who make hot gazpacho jokes, an actual hot gazpacho from Spain.

I'm not saying that this recipe will stop purists from arguing, but it will produce something like what I've been served in small Spanish bars.

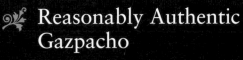

Reasonably Authentic Gazpacho

Makes 4 servings

1 cup stale bread, cut into
    thumbnail-size cubes
2 cups chopped ripe tomatoes
1 cup chopped cucumber
    plus extra for garnish
1 cup chopped red or yellow bell
    pepper plus extra for garnish
1 clove garlic
1 tablespoon sherry vinegar
2 tablespoons olive oil
1 teaspoon salt
1/2 teaspoon freshly ground
    black pepper
1 tablespoon chopped parsley

1. Soak the bread in water for a few moments, and then squeeze it dry.

2. Put the soaked bread, tomatoes, cucumber, bell pepper, garlic, vinegar, oil, salt, and ground pepper in a food processor, and mix until everything is both liquefied and well distributed. Refrigerate.

3. To serve, put a couple of ice cubes in a tall glass, fill it with the gazpacho mixture, and garnish it with parsley, cucumber, and pepper.

If blending their vegetables into a delicious cold liquid isn't enough to get your family to eat them, we'll go one or two steps further: Spice them up with chili peppers, and put a nice scoop of sour cream on top.

 ## Southwestern-Style Spicy Gazpacho

Makes 4 servings

2 cups chopped fresh tomatoes

1 cup chopped cucumber

1 cup chopped bell pepper

1 fresh jalapeño pepper,
    stem removed

1/4 cup chopped onion

1/4 cup fresh cilantro

2 cloves peeled, fresh garlic

2 tablespoons lemon juice

1 teaspoon ground cumin

1 cup sour cream

1. Combine the tomatoes, cucumber, pepper, jalapeño, onion, cilantro, garlic, lemon juice, and cumin in a blender, and purée until smooth.

2. To serve, put a couple of ice cubes in a tall glass and pour in the liquid. Garnish with a scoop of sour cream.

This is the dish that defies all the jokers: hot gazpacho.
Is it the real thing? Well . . . kind of. It's as much a cousin
of ratatouille as of that cold tomato-and-bread soup.
But no matter what its lineage, it's worth making.

❦ Spanish-Style Rabbit and Tomato Stew (Gazpacho Manchego)

Makes 6 servings

2 tablespoons olive oil

1 whole rabbit* (about
    2 to 2 ½ pounds),
    cut into pieces

2 whole heads of garlic,
    unseparated but
    cut in half

1 cup chopped onion

2 cups chopped ripe
    tomatoes

1 cup chopped red
    bell pepper

2 cups chicken broth

2 bay leaves

1 cup toasted stale bread,
    torn into thumbnail-
    size pieces

1 teaspoon sea salt

1/2 teaspoon freshly
    ground black pepper

*Yes, you can substitute
pork loin or chicken.

1. Heat the oil in a large pot over medium heat, and sauté the rabbit pieces and garlic heads until the meat is well browned.

2. Add the onion, tomatoes, and pepper, and cook, stirring, until they're softened and start to brown, about 20 minutes.

3. Stir in the broth and bay leaves and bring to a boil for 1 minute. Lower the heat to medium-low and let the mixture simmer covered, occasionally stirring, for 30 minutes.

4. Mix in the bread, salt, and pepper, and continue to cook until the bread has dissolved and thickened the liquid into a sauce, about 15 more minutes.

5. Discard the heads of garlic. Serve hot.

4. meat, fish, and poultry

No . . . this dish bears no resemblance to any Chinese or Chinese American recipe. But that's what it's called on menus all over the country. Serve this as a stew or instead of a soup

American Chop Suey

Makes 4 servings

6 quarts water

2 tablespoons salt

1/2 pound elbow macaroni

1/2 recipe (about 3 cups) Sloppy Joes (page 104)

1. Pour the water into a large pot, add the salt, and bring to a boil over high heat.

2. Stir in the macaroni, lower the heat to medium, and simmer for 8 minutes or until the macaroni is just a little bit under-cooked. Drain.

3. Return the drained macaroni to the pot and combine with the Sloppy Joes. Let the mixture simmer uncovered over low heat for 5 minutes or until the flavors combine. Serve warm.

What is that little ethnic restaurant down the street serving? Italian has been around so long it isn't even considered "ethnic" anymore. Latin American and Asian cuisines are common enough to attract the attention of both average eaters and upscale restaurant critics. So what about African, then? Ethiopian and Moroccan are getting more popular, and foods from Nigeria, Gambia, and Sierra Leone are starting to appear in local storefronts that once held pizza joints or bagel shops.

This recipe is an African basic that gets its distinctive flavor from two ingredients very commonly found in American kitchens but never, ever combined. Will you be the one to finally mix them together?

African Chicken in Tomato and Peanut Sauce

Makes 4 servings

2 tablespoons peanut oil

1 whole chicken (about 3 pounds),
    cut into pieces

1 teaspoon ground chili pepper

2 cups sliced onion

3 cloves garlic, sliced

2 cups canned crushed tomatoes
    or *passata* (page 20)

1 cup smooth peanut butter

1/2 teaspoon salt

1/2 teaspoon freshly ground black pepper

1. Heat the oil and chicken pieces in a large skillet over medium-high heat, and cook until the skin of the chicken is nicely browned, about 3 minutes per side. Set the browned pieces aside. (You may have to do this in several batches to make sure the chicken browns completely.)

2. Add the ground chili, onions, and garlic to the pan and cook, stirring frequently, until the onions soften and the bits of chicken that stuck to the pan have loosened and combined with the onion, about 10 minutes.

3. Reduce the heat to medium-low, and mix in the tomatoes, peanut butter, salt, and pepper. Stir until combined into a smooth sauce. Return the browned chicken to the pan and simmer covered, occasionally stirring, until the chicken is completely cooked, about 40 minutes. Serve immediately over rice.

This dish with classic Middle Eastern seasonings works perfectly with fish fillets like tilapia, cod, or even salmon.

🌿 Braised Fish with a Middle Eastern Tomato Sauce
Makes 2 servings

2 tablespoons olive oil

1/2 teaspoon dried thyme

1/2 teaspoon ground cumin

1/2 teaspoon ground coriander

1/4 teaspoon ground cardamom

1/2 cup chopped onion

2 cloves garlic, crushed and chopped

3 tablespoons chopped parsley

2 cups canned crushed tomatoes
   or *passata* (page 20)

1/2 teaspoon salt

1/2 teaspoon freshly ground black pepper

1 teaspoon brown sugar

1 cup water

2 tilapia fillets (about 6 to 8 ounces each)*

*Substitute cod or other fish if you prefer.

1. Heat the oil in a flat-bottomed skillet over medium heat. Mix in the thyme, cumin, coriander, and cardamom, and cook, stirring, for about 1 minute or until you can smell the spices.

2. Add the onion, garlic, and parsley, and cook, occasionally stirring, for about 15 minutes or until the onion is tender and translucent.

3. Mix in the tomatoes, salt, pepper, sugar, and water. Reduce heat to medium-low, and let the mixture simmer uncovered, occasionally stirring, for about 10 minutes or until the raw taste is gone from the tomato.

4. Add the fish fillets and cover with sauce. Cook about 20 more minutes or until the fish is cooked through. Serve immediately.

Tomatoes aren't a staple in Chinese cooking, but they do show up in some Cantonese noodle-shop classics.

 ## Beef and Tomato Chow Mein

Makes 4 servings

2 teaspoons cornstarch

1 tablespoon Chinese cooking
   wine or sherry

2 tablespoons soy sauce

1/2 pound beef fillet, cut into
   thin strips

2 quarts water

6 ounces chow mein noodles

2 tablespoons peanut oil

1 tablespoon black bean garlic sauce

1 tablespoon finely minced ginger

1 cup sliced onions

1/2 cup peas

2 cups tomato wedges

2 teaspoons sesame oil

1. Mix the cornstarch, cooking wine, and soy sauce in a large bowl. Add the beef strips and toss so that the meat is well coated. Marinate in the refrigerator for at least 30 minutes.

2. Bring the water to a boil and immerse the chow mein noodles. Lower the heat to medium and cook for about 3 minutes or until the noodles are tender. Rinse them in cold water, drain, and set aside.

3. Have the remaining ingredients within easy reach of your stove. Heat a wok on your hottest burner over high heat. Add the oil, garlic sauce, and ginger. Stir continuously for about 1 minute.

4. Add the onions and stir continuously until they're soft and translucent—about 8 minutes on a home stove, a bit less on a hotter commercial one.

5. Mix in the marinated beef, the peas, and the tomatoes, cooking and stirring the mixture for about 5 minutes or until the beef is cooked.

6. Add the noodles and toss vigorously. Make sure all the ingredients are evenly distributed and the noodles are coated with sauce. Finally, add the sesame oil, give the mixture a few more tosses, and remove from the heat. Serve immediately.

Is this beef stewed in yet another kind of tomato sauce? Well . . . yes, this time with just a touch of Latin American spice. Serve this up with yellow rice and tortillas.

 ## Beef Stewed in Tomato Sauce (Carne Guisada)

Makes 4 servings

1 tablespoon olive oil

1 teaspoon ground cumin

1 teaspoon dried red pepper
   flakes

3 cloves garlic, crushed

1 cup chopped green bell pepper

1 pound chuck steak cut
   into 1-inch cubes

2 cups canned crushed tomatoes
   or *passata* (page 20)

1/2 teaspoon salt

1/2 teaspoon freshly ground
   black pepper

1 cup water

1. Heat the oil, cumin, pepper flakes, garlic, and bell pepper in a heavy pot over medium heat, and cook, stirring frequently, for about 15 minutes or until the bell pepper becomes tender.

2. Add the meat, and cook, stirring, for about 15 minutes or until the meat browns.

3. Mix in the tomatoes, salt, ground pepper, and water, and give it a few stirs to make sure the ingredients are well combined. Reduce the heat to medium-low, and simmer covered, occasionally stirring, for about 2 hours or until the beef is very tender. Serve warm.

With plenty of spice going for it, this chicken dish should be much more popular than it is.

Bolivian Chicken with Spicy Hot Sauce (Sajta)

Makes 4 servings

2 tablespoons peanut oil

1 tablespoon dried hot red pepper flakes

1 teaspoon dried oregano

2 teaspoons ground cumin

1 teaspoon salt

1/2 teaspoon freshly ground
    black pepper

2 cups chopped onions

6 cloves garlic

1 whole chicken (about 2 to
    3 pounds) cut into pieces

2 cups canned whole peeled tomatoes

1/4 cup chopped parsley

1 cup chopped green bell pepper

2 cups peeled and cubed yucca

1. Heat the oil, pepper flakes, oregano, cumin, salt, and ground pepper in a Dutch oven over medium heat. Cook, stirring, until the spices are coated with oil and are fragrant, about 1 minute.

2. Mix in the onions and garlic, and continue to cook, occasionally stirring, until the onion is very tender, about 15 minutes.

3. Add the chicken. Stir to make sure the chicken skin has contact with the bottom of the pan and isn't just sitting on the onions. Cook, turning the chicken pieces over a few times and making certain they've completely browned, about 15 minutes.

4. Mix in the tomatoes, parsley, bell pepper, and yucca. If there isn't enough liquid to barely cover all the ingredients, add water until there is. Reduce the heat to medium-low, and simmer covered until the chicken is completely cooked and the yucca is tender, about 45 minutes. Serve warm.

Chicken Cacciatore is one of those Italian American dishes that varies so much, you have to take sides to publish a recipe. I like my chicken with the bone in, my herbs dried, and my peppers red. That still leaves a thousand variations. . . .

❧ Chicken Cacciatore

Makes 6 servings

2 tablespoons olive oil

2 teaspoons dried oregano

1 cup chopped onion

4 cloves garlic, chopped

1 whole chicken (about 2 to 3
   pounds), cut into pieces

2 1/2 cups sliced fresh
   mushrooms

1 cup chopped red bell pepper

3 1/2 cups canned crushed
   tomatoes or *passata* (page 20)

1/2 teaspoon salt

1/2 teaspoon freshly ground
   black pepper

1. Heat the oil, oregano, onion, and garlic in a Dutch oven over medium heat, and cook, stirring, until the onion is translucent and begins to brown at the edges, about 10 minutes.

2. Add the chicken and continue cooking until the skin is well browned, about 20 minutes. Turn several times to help it cook evenly.

3. Add the mushrooms and bell pepper and cook, stirring, until the pepper pieces are tender, about 10 minutes.

4. Mix in the tomato, salt, and ground pepper, and reduce the heat to medium-low. Simmer covered, occasionally stirring, until the chicken is cooked through to the bone and all the raw taste is gone from the tomato, about 40 more minutes. Serve warm.

Is this dish Middle Eastern? Neapolitan? I've even seen similar recipes labeled as Hungarian. Whatever it is, it's a great way to serve eggs without reminding people of breakfast.

🌿 Eggs Poached in Tomato Sauce

Makes 2 servings

2 tablespoons olive oil
2 anchovy fillets
1/2 teaspoon dried
   oregano
1/4 teaspoon dried
   red pepper flakes
1/2 cup chopped
   onion
2 cloves garlic, crushed
   and chopped

2 cups canned crushed
   tomatoes or
   passata (page 20)
4 eggs
2 tablespoons
   chopped parsley
1 tablespoon grated
   Parmesan cheese

1. Heat the oil and anchovies in a skillet over medium-low heat, and cook, stirring, until the anchovies have dissolved in the oil, about 3 minutes.

2. Mix in the oregano and pepper, making sure they're coated with the oil.

3. Add the onion and garlic, and cook, occasionally stirring, until the onion is translucent and tender, about 15 minutes.

4. Add the tomatoes and simmer covered, occasionally stirring, until the raw tomato taste is gone and the onion, herb, and tomato flavors have combined, about 10 minutes.

5. Break the eggs over the cooking tomato sauce. Cover the pot so that the heat and steam coming off the tomato sauce cooks the eggs.

6. When the whites have pretty much cooked through, about 10 minutes, spoon some of the tomato sauce over the cooking eggs, and cover again. Cook until the yolks are done, about 4 more minutes.

7. To serve, use a spatula to place the eggs on plates, spoon sauce over them, and then sprinkle with the parsley and cheese.

There's a point where all those tomato dishes start looking like one big pot of red glop. When you've reached it—and still have lots of tomatoes on hand—try this.

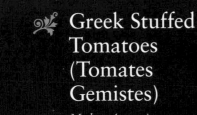

Greek Stuffed Tomatoes (Tomates Gemistes)

Makes 4 servings

4 large ripe tomatoes

1 tablespoon olive oil
    plus oil for baking dish

1 cup chopped onion

2 cloves garlic, crushed
    and chopped

1/2 pound ground lamb

1/2 cup uncooked white rice

2 tablespoons pine nuts

1/4 cup raisins

1/2 teaspoon salt

1 cup chicken broth

1. Cut the tops off the tomatoes. Use a spoon—one of those serrated grapefruit spoons is great here—to hollow out the bodies. Reserve everything—bodies, tops, and pulp—separately.

2. Heat the oil, onion, and garlic in a skillet over medium heat and cook, stirring, for 15 minutes or until the onion begins to turn golden at the edges.

3. Add the lamb and 1 cup of the reserved tomato pulp and continue cooking for about 20 minutes or until the meat is completely browned. Use the back of a wooden spoon to break up any clumps.

4. Mix in the rice, pine nuts, raisins, salt, and broth. Give it a few stirs, lower the heat to medium-low, and simmer covered for 20 minutes or until the rice has absorbed all the liquid. Remove from the heat and set aside.

5. Preheat your oven to 325 degrees.

6. Oil a baking dish. Fill the hollow tomato bodies with the meat mixture and stand them on end in the baking dish. They should stand up nicely; if they don't, use a sharp knife to slice a bit off the bottom. Place the reserved tops back on the tomatoes.

7. Brush the stuffed tomatoes with olive oil, and bake for 30 minutes or until the tomato is completely cooked and the meat inside is hot. Serve warm.

Burgoo is yet another one of those recipes that nobody can agree on. Some people insist it has to have mutton—or even squirrel. But since you're not likely to find either in your local supermarket, we'll stick with the basics. It's still Burgoo— a meat-and-vegetable stew in a roux-based tomato sauce.

🌿 Stewed Meats and Vegetables (Burgoo)

Makes 6 servings

1/4 pound bacon,
    cut into 1-inch pieces
1 teaspoon freshly ground
    black pepper
1 teaspoon chili flakes
1 pound boneless chicken
    breast or thigh, cut into
    1/2-inch pieces
1 pound lamb stew meat,
    cut into 1/2-inch pieces
1/4 cup all-purpose flour
2 cups water
1 cup finely chopped potato

3 cloves garlic, crushed
    and chopped
1 cup corn kernels
1 cup sliced okra
2 cups canned crushed
    tomatoes or *passata*
    (page 20)
2 tablespoons
    Worcestershire sauce
1 bay leaf
1 tablespoon brown sugar
1 teaspoon salt

1. Cook the bacon in a large pot over medium heat. When it begins to brown, add the pepper, chili flakes, chicken, and lamb. Cook, occasionally stirring, until all the meat is well browned, about 20 minutes. Remove the meat from the pot and set aside.

2. Add the flour to the pot and stir until a thick paste forms and turns a golden color, about 5 minutes. Then mix in the water, 1/4 cup at a time, and keep stirring until you have a smooth liquid.

3. Return the meats to the pot and add the potato, garlic, corn, okra, tomatoes, Worcestershire sauce, bay leaf, and brown sugar. Lower the heat to medium-low and simmer uncovered until the lamb is tender, about 2 hours.

4. Taste the sauce and add the salt if needed. Serve warm.

So who doesn't love meatballs? Indeed, what cuisine doesn't have them? This recipe features both a tomato-flavored meatball and a tomato-yogurt sauce. Serve kofta warm over rice or couscous—and make sure that nobody eats the whole cinnamon sticks, cloves, or cardamom pods.

Tomato-Flavored Meatballs in a Tomato-Yogurt Sauce (Kofta)

Makes 4 servings

Meatballs

1 pound ground lamb*

1 egg

4 cloves garlic, crushed and chopped

1 tablespoon finely chopped fresh ginger

2 tablespoons finely chopped fresh green chilies

2 teaspoons tomato paste

1 teaspoon ground cumin

2 tablespoons chopped parsley

1/2 teaspoon salt

1/2 teaspoon freshly ground black pepper

Oil for frying (optional)

*Ground beef can be substituted

1. Combine the lamb, egg, garlic, ginger, chilies, tomato paste, cumin, parsley, salt, and ground pepper in a large bowl, and mix until everything is well combined. Form into golf ball–size meatballs. Refrigerate until ready to cook.

2. Fry the meatballs in a well-oiled skillet over medium heat. They'll be ready when the outsides are browned and the meat is just cooked in the center.

Sauce

2 tablespoons peanut oil

2 cinnamon sticks

6 cloves

6 cardamom pods

1 teaspoon ground cumin

1 tablespoon ground
    coriander

1 teaspoon ground
    turmeric

1 teaspoon red
    chili powder

1 teaspoon garam
    masala powder

1/2 cup chopped onion

2 cups canned, crushed
    tomatoes or
    passata (page 20)

2 cups plain yogurt

1. In a saucepan large enough to hold all the ingredients plus the meatballs, heat the oil, cinnamon sticks, cloves, cardamom, cumin, coriander, turmeric, chili powder, and garam masala over medium heat. Cook, stirring, until you can smell the spices, about 1 minute.

2. Reduce the heat to medium-low, add the onion, and keep cooking, occasionally stirring, until the onion turns translucent and begins to brown at the edges, about 10 minutes.

3. Mix in the tomatoes and yogurt, making sure all the seasonings are well combined. Add the meatballs and simmer until they're cooked all the way through, about 30 more minutes.

The Tomato Vendors: Horst Farm Market

Each time I asked a question, the two Mennonite girls by the cash register broke into side-splitting laughter. I wasn't trying to be funny; indeed, I thought my questions were serious, but at the Horst Farm Market in East Earl Pennsylvania, holding up a head of fresh garlic and asking, "Does this come from China?" is the height of hilarity.

When I then picked up a couple of bunches of broccoli, one of the girls almost shrieked, "That's from Thailand! That's from a country farther away than Thailand whose name we can't even think of!" And they once again dissolved into laughter.

You might have thought that the global food trade had penetrated every corner of the food business, but not this one. This is an outpost of local food for people who believe that "local" is a practical matter, not one related to politics, environmental issues, or any philosophy at all.

Paul W. Horst doesn't just sell produce. There are traditional Pennsylvania Dutch baked goods like whoopee and shoofly pies, a few bulk items like flour and soup mix, and even a deli counter where Mr. Horst or the girls will make sandwiches for you. And of course, there's the coffeepot that's always ready for whoever needs a cup.

More to the point is what Mr. Horst *doesn't* sell. At Horst Farm Market, there aren't twenty varieties of tomatoes to confuse you, just four: red and yellow beefsteaks, plums for sauce, and a few errant baskets of cherry. (OK, there are green too, but they're the same as the red—just picked earlier.) There are no heirloom—or as Mr. Horst calls them, "fancy"—tomatoes at all. In fact, there's nothing fancy here. Broccoli is green heads, onions are red or yellow, and the only fresh herb is basil.

The regulars don't expect much in the way of variety, but each item they choose has to be the best possible. And they have to know who grew it—not because it might otherwise be from Thailand, but because it might have been raised by somebody they saw in church the week before.

Passing through the other day (it's not that far from the Pennsylvania Turnpike, if you know the way), I picked up a basket of perfect yellow tomatoes. Paired with some local cheese, they made great sandwiches—and a fresh pasta sauce (page 20) and some gazpacho (page 75), too. The cost? A buck and a quarter for all of them . . . and there was no extra charge for the laughing cashiers.

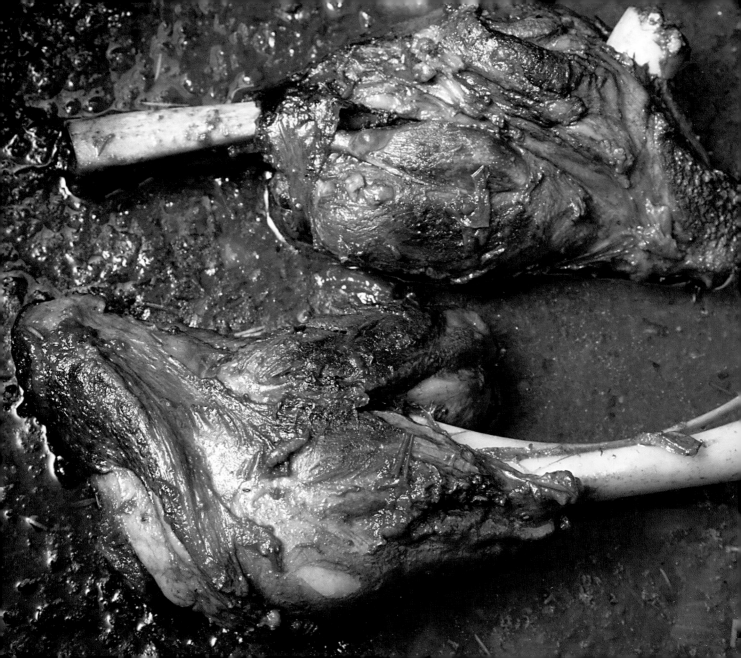

When did this cut of meat become commonplace? They used to be hard to find, but now lamb shanks are suddenly turning up everywhere. Serve this dish with rice, potatoes, or couscous.

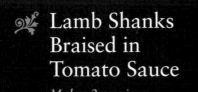

Lamb Shanks Braised in Tomato Sauce

Makes 2 servings

2 tablespoons olive oil

2 lamb shanks

1 teaspoon dried oregano

1 teaspoon dried rosemary

1 cup chopped onion

3 cloves garlic, chopped

1 cup red wine

2 cups canned crushed tomatoes
  or *passata* (page 20)

1 teaspoon salt

1/2 teaspoon freshly ground
  black pepper

1. Heat the oil and lamb shanks in a Dutch oven over high heat and cook until they're browned fairly evenly, about 30 minutes. Lots of brown bits should be stuck to the bottom of the pot. Don't worry; they give great flavor. Remove the meat from the pot and set aside.

2. Reduce the heat to medium-low and add the oregano and rosemary. Cook, stirring, until the spices are coated with oil, about 30 seconds. Mix in the onion and garlic and cook until the onion turns completely translucent, about 15 minutes.

3. Remove the pot from the heat and add the wine, tomatoes, salt, and pepper. Give it a few good stirs and return the pot to medium-low heat.

4. When the liquid is simmering, add the browned lamb shanks. They don't need to be covered with sauce, just sitting in it. Cover and cook, occasionally stirring—every 20 minutes or so is OK— until the meat is falling off the bone, about 2 hours.

Variation: If you let the lamb cook for an additional hour, the meat will fall completely away from the bones. Use tongs to remove the bones, and serve as a stew.

I would like to think of Portuguese as my favorite Mediterranean cuisine. It's got great vegetables, seafood, wine, and grilling. But there's one problem: Portugal isn't on the Mediterranean. This is still worth cooking, though. . . . Serve over rice.

Portuguese Pork and Clam Stew (Ameijoas na Cataplana)

Makes 4 servings

2 tablespoons olive oil

1/2 pound Portuguese
    Linguica sausage,* sliced

2 cups chopped onions

1 cup coarsely chopped fresh
    bell pepper

6 cloves of garlic, crushed
    and chopped

1 pound boneless pork loin,
    cut into 1-inch cubes

1 cup dry white wine

2 bay leaves

2 cups coarsely chopped
    fresh tomatoes

1/2 cup chopped parsley

1/2 teaspoon salt

1/2 teaspoon freshly
    ground black pepper

2 dozen littleneck clams

*Substitute kielbasa or a
similar smoked sausage
if this is unavailable.

1. Heat the oil, sausage, and onion in a Dutch oven over medium heat (*cataplana* means a "clam-shaped Dutch oven" in Portuguese), and cook, occasionally stirring, until the onion is tender and translucent, about 15 minutes.

2. Mix in the bell pepper and garlic, and cook until the garlic is tender, about 20 minutes.

3. Add the pork, and cook, occasionally stirring, until the meat is browned, about 15 minutes.

4. Add the wine, bay leaves, tomatoes, and parsley. Reduce the heat to medium-low, and simmer uncovered, occasionally stirring, until one-quarter of the liquid has evaporated, about 45 minutes.

5. Taste the sauce and add the salt if needed. (It's impossible to know in advance and depends on how much salt is in the sausage.) Then add the ground pepper, and stir a few times to mix the spices in.

6. Scatter the clams on top of the sausage mixture. Cover, and let cook for 20 minutes. At this point, the shells should be open; discard those that are still closed. Serve immediately.

In my experience (more hard won than you can possibly imagine), two things will make or break salt-cod dishes: the piece of fish you choose and how well you do at rehydration. As far as choosing goes, pick a piece that's thick, boneless, and white or light-ivory colored. Unless you're an expert in the genre, skip the pieces with bone or those cheaper, thin ones. They're great for somebody but not for us.

Salt Cod Braised in Tomato Sauce

Makes 2 servings

1 pound salt-cod fillet

3 tablespoons olive oil

1 teaspoon freshly ground black pepper

4 cloves garlic, crushed and chopped

1/2 cup chopped onion

1 teaspoon dried oregano

1 tablespoon capers, rinsed and drained

2 tablespoons pitted chopped olives

2 cups canned crushed tomatoes
    or *passata* (page 20)

1 cup dry white wine

1. Wash the fish in cold running water, rubbing it a bit with your fingers to remove all the surface salt. Lay the fillet in a nonmetallic dish filled with water and refrigerate. The fish needs to soak for a minimum of 3 days, changing the water every morning and evening. When you're ready to cook, pat the fish dry with paper towels and then proceed.

2. Cut the fish up into 2-inch pieces and sprinkle with the ground pepper. In a heavy skillet, sauté the fish in the oil over medium heat. Turn the pieces frequently, making sure they don't burn. When they're lightly browned, remove them from the pan and set aside.

3. Lower the heat to medium-low, and in the same pan add the garlic, onion, and oregano. Cook, stirring, until the onion turns translucent and begins to brown at the edges, about 25 minutes.

4. Mix in the capers, olives, tomatoes, and wine, and bring to a simmer. Return the browned fish pieces to the pan and cover well with sauce. Continue simmering, occasionally stirring, until roughly one-quarter of the liquid has evaporated, about 40 minutes. Serve warm.

Note: If you cheated on any of these steps, this dish will remind you by being too salty. Don't skimp! Make sure your fish is properly soaked—a taste of the soaking water should have almost no trace of saltiness. If it's still salty, give the fish another day in water.

Sloppy Joes, sometimes also called "loose meat," are a mild and easy version of chili (page 109)—a stew of meat, tomatoes, spices, and perhaps something else. During my childhood, it was served over burger buns—which you can certainly do—but I think that these days I'd prefer it in a bowl. It's also great over a hot dog instead of chili, or . . . ??

 ## Sloppy Joes
Makes 6 servings

2 tablespoons olive oil

2 pounds ground chuck*

1 teaspoon paprika

1 teaspoon mustard
      powder

1 teaspoon ground cumin

1 teaspoon dried
      oregano

1 tablespoon Worcester-
      shire sauce

2 cups chopped onions

4 cloves garlic, crushed
      and chopped

1 cup chopped yellow
      bell pepper

2 cups canned, crushed
      tomatoes
      or *passata* (page 20)

1 teaspoon salt

1/2 teaspoon freshly
      ground black pepper

*Don't use the more
expensive stuff—it will
be dry and tasteless.

1. Heat the oil, meat, paprika, mustard powder, cumin, and oregano in a heavy pot over medium heat and cook, stirring, until the meat begins to turn from gray to brown, about 15 minutes.

2. Add the Worcestershire, onion, garlic, and bell pepper and cook, occasionally stirring, until the onions are translucent and starting to brown, about 30 minutes.

3. Mix in the tomatoes, salt, and pepper, lower the heat a bit, and simmer until the flavors are blended and about one-quarter of the liquid has evaporated, about 20 minutes. The dish is ready when a thick sauce has formed and there's no raw tomato taste at all. Serve warm.

Wasn't it just a few decades ago that nobody at all ate squid? Aren't there still a whole bunch of people who'll eat it when it's called "calamari" but not when we use that icky English word? Serve this with spaghetti or rice.

Squid Rings Stewed in Tomato Sauce

Makes 4 servings

2 tablespoons olive oil

4 anchovy fillets

2 teaspoons dried oregano

1 teaspoon hot pepper flakes

5 cloves garlic, crushed and chopped

1 pound squid rings*

1 cup chopped yellow bell pepper

1 cup chopped red bell pepper

1 cup dry white table wine

2 cups canned crushed tomatoes or *passata* (page 20)

1/2 teaspoon salt

1/2 teaspoon freshly ground black pepper

*Buy frozen squid rings from a shop with obviously high turnover. If you choose to use fresh, make sure that the squid hasn't been previously frozen and really is as fresh as claimed.

1. Heat the olive oil and anchovies in a skillet over medium heat and cook, stirring, until the anchovies have dissolved, about 3 minutes.

2. Mix in the oregano, pepper flakes, and garlic, and cook until the garlic begins to brown at the edges and the spices are coated with oil, about 5 minutes.

3. Add the squid rings, yellow pepper, and red pepper, and cook, occasionally stirring, until the peppers start to become tender, about 5 minutes.

4. Remove the skillet from the heat and mix in the wine, tomatoes, salt, and ground pepper. (This avoids those nasty flare-ups that happen when wine and flame meet.)

5. Put the squid mixture back on medium-low heat, and simmer until roughly one-third of the liquid has evaporated and thickened into a sauce, about 60 minutes. Serve warm.

There are people who eat sushi three times a week and know how to make *udon* from scratch but don't eat stir-fried Japanese dishes. That's a shame because it's a genre that deserves to be more well known. Serve this over rice.

 Japanese Beef and Tomato Stir-Fry

Makes 4 servings

1/4 cup soy sauce

1/4 cup sake

1/2 pound shredded or thinly
　　sliced beef

2 tablespoons cornstarch

2 tablespoons peanut oil

1 tablespoon minced
　　fresh ginger

1 cup coarsely chopped onion

1 cup coarsely chopped
　　red bell pepper

2 cups tomato wedges

1 teaspoon sugar

1. Mix the soy sauce and sake together in a medium nonmetallic bowl. Add the beef and combine, making sure that every bit is coated with liquid. Marinate in the refrigerator for at least 2 hours. (It can be left all day if need be.) When ready to cook, drain off the liquid, sprinkle the meat with the cornstarch, and toss to make sure the cornstarch coats the meat evenly.

2. Heat a wok over very high heat and add the oil. When it begins to smoke, mix in the ginger and cook, stirring, for 10 seconds (I count out loud). Add the beef and stir-fry until it's just cooked through, about 1 minute. Remove the beef from the wok and set aside.

3. Keep that wok on high heat, and mix in the onion, pepper, tomatoes, and sugar and cook, stirring—they don't call this "stir-frying" for nothing—until the onion is browned at the edges and the pepper is tender, about 2 minutes.

4. Return the beef to the wok, and give the whole thing a couple more stirs to make sure it's all combined. Serve immediately.

I often wonder why Moroccan cuisine is so obscure here. The flavors are intense, the techniques are fairly simple, and the ingredients are easy to find. Note that the cooking method—with no pre-browning of meat or onions—is just a bit different than typical European-style stews. Serve this dish with rice or couscous.

 ## Tajine of Lamb and Tomatoes

Makes 6 servings

2 pounds lamb stewing meat

4 cloves garlic, crushed and chopped

1 cup chopped onion

1 teaspoon salt

2 teaspoons turmeric

2 cups canned whole peeled tomatoes

2 cups coarsely chopped zucchini

2 cups coarsely chopped fresh pumpkin

1/4 cup raisins

3 cups water

1. Preheat your oven to 325 degrees.

2. Combine the lamb, garlic, onion, salt, turmeric, tomatoes, zucchini, pumpkin, raisins, and water together in a Dutch oven. Stir to dissolve the spices and combine the ingredients, cover tightly, and bake, occasionally stirring, for 3 hours or until the meat and pumpkin are very tender. Serve warm.

Yes . . . there's New York and bagels, Boston and baked beans (page 173), and Texas and chili—foods that are so deeply associated with places that it's hard to separate them. Of course, when you start to explore what makes Texas chili special, you wind up with answers (especially if—like me—you have a New York accent and a New Jersey home address) like "Texas chili is special because it's better" or "Texas chili is the one without beans."

Other components seem to come and go. When I was thumbing my way across west Texas in 1978, the chili I enjoyed the most was braised in beer, but this practice has almost vanished—except here. And with all the great beers available these days, it would be a shame to not cook *something* with them.

I've always liked rice and beans on the side, but cornbread is a bit more traditional.

✿ Texas Home-Style Chili

Makes 6 servings

2 tablespoons shortening

2 pounds beef chuck, cut into
cubes the size of dice*

2 teaspoons ground cumin

1 teaspoon dried oregano

1 teaspoon paprika

1 teaspoon salt

1/2 teaspoon freshly ground
black pepper

2 cups chopped onions

6 cloves garlic, crushed
and chopped

2 jalapeño peppers, stems
and seeds removed and
finely chopped

1/2 cup chopped poblano
pepper

3 cups pale ale (two 12-ounce
bottles)

1 cup canned crushed tomatoes
or *passata* (page 20)

*Texans may use ground beef
in private, but if you want to
do it right, use the chuck.

1. Melt the shortening in a heavy pot over medium-high heat. Brown the beef cubes in it, remove them from the pot when they're done, and set aside. At this point, the meat should be really brown, not just gray. And don't worry about any of it sticking to the pot; it will come right off a little later on.

2. Lower the heat to medium, and add the cumin, oregano, paprika, salt, and ground pepper and cook, stirring, until you can really smell the spices frying, about 1 minute.

3. Mix in the onion, garlic, jalapeños, and poblanos, and stir vigorously until all the brown bits of meat stuck on the bottom of the pot loosen and combine with the onions, about 5 minutes.

4. Remove the pot from the heat. Add the browned meat, beer, and tomatoes, and put the pot back on medium-low. Simmer, occasionally stirring, until the meat is very tender and the sauce is thick, about 2 hours. Serve hot.

Competition Chili

If you watch enough TV, you'll certainly stumble on one or another of those chili cook-offs. You know—the ones with teams in tents cooking on camping stoves while beauty pageants, country music concerts, and enthusiastic crowds in cowboy hats swirl around them. Now, I'm a sucker for these programs and can watch them for hours, but I have to confess that before I began my tomato odyssey, I'd tasted dozens of different kinds of chili, but not this, the competition brew, the most celebrated of all.

How is this chili different from what we normally get in diners or over hot dogs?

I dove into the research with great enthusiasm. I already knew that no beans were ever used and that most competitors—but by no means all—eschewed ground meat for finely diced pieces of steak. Still, what besides cumin and chili powder were they adding to the pot?

I went to a competition in North Plainfield, New Jersey, to find out, strolling between the contestant stations and chatting with them as they cooked and stirred. The pressure was on, though, and nobody really wanted to talk. Instead, they were concentrating on turning in their "specimens." (I would have used a word like "sample" myself, but "specimen" seemed to be the descriptor of choice that day.)

Before I knew it—and before I had the chance to tell anybody that I was a food writer—I was handed a clipboard and pressed into duty as a judge. Soon I joined a bunch of other nameless middle-aged men and was sniffing, tasting, and carefully examining chili.

What did the competitors cook?

About half of them seemed to have used hamburger meat, which made their chili taste like mush. For the sort of long cooking that the seasonings needed to develop properly, small cubes of beef work best, and the "specimens" made that way stood out. All were really mild. I overheard other people mentioning spice and heat as they ate, but I didn't detect it at all. Even the best had a salty, powdery taste from ingredients like garlic salt and bullion cubes, and none gave me the thrill that I've gotten from a "bowl of red" in a small-town Texas café.

Would I have been more pleased at a competition in Chili Country? I don't know. Championship recipes call for loads of powders and salts and are low on things like fresh onions, garlic, and peppers—the true bearers of flavor and richness.

I never found out who the winner was. After tasting all that chili, I turned in my score sheet and headed home to fine-tune my own recipe.

This dish is pretty basic in a way: potatoes, tomatoes, some bell pepper, and a bit of meat. It adds up to something really delicious, though, and is very much worth trying.

 ## Turkish Potato, Lamb, and Tomato Casserole (Patates Oturtmasi)

Makes 6 servings

1/4 cup olive oil plus
    2 tablespoons for frying
3 cups sliced potatoes
1 teaspoon plus 1/2 teaspoon salt
1 teaspoon freshly ground
    black pepper, divided
3 cloves garlic, sliced thin
2 tablespoons tomato paste
2 cups chopped onions
1/2 pound ground lamb
1 cup chopped green bell pepper
2 cups sliced fresh tomatoes

1. Preheat your oven to 350 degrees.

2. Use some of the olive oil, oil a 9 by 13-inch baking dish, and lay the slices of potato out on it. Brush the potato with the remaining oil, and season with 1 teaspoon of the salt and 1/2 teaspoon of the pepper.

2. Bake until the potatoes begin to brown, about 30 minutes. Remove from the oven and set aside.

3. Put the 2 tablespoons of frying oil, the garlic, tomato paste, and onions in a skillet and cook, stirring, over medium heat until the onions become tender and start to brown at the edges, about 15 minutes.

4. Add the lamb and bell pepper, cooking until the meat is browned and the pepper is tender, about 20 minutes.

5. Spread the cooked meat mixture over the baked potatoes, distribute the tomato slices over the meat, and season with the remaining 1/2 teaspoon of salt and 1/2 teaspoon of ground pepper. Return to the oven and bake until the tomatoes are fully cooked, about 30 minutes. Serve warm.

5. rice and pasta

It seems that every West African country claims Jollof Rice as its own. "Jollof," also called "Benachin," means "one pot" in the Jollof language. Jollof Rice is a popular dish throughout that region and is a great switch from Spanish Rice (page 125) or Rice Pilaf (page 131).

Jollof Rice

Makes 4 Servings

1 tablespoon peanut oil

2 tablespoons dried
   shrimp

1/2 teaspoon freshly
   ground black
   pepper

1/2 teaspoon salt

1 tablespoon chopped
   fresh ginger

4 cloves garlic, crushed
   and chopped

1 cup chopped onion

1 cup long-grain white
   rice

1 tablespoon tomato
   paste

1 cup chopped fresh
   tomatoes

3 cups chicken broth

1/2 cup diced green
   bell pepper

1/2 cup chopped string
   beans

1 hard-cooked egg,
   sliced

1. Heat the oil, shrimp, ground pepper, salt, ginger, and garlic in a heavy pot over medium heat, and cook, stirring, until everything is coated with oil and the garlic begins to turn translucent, about 5 minutes.

2. Mix in the onion and cook, occasionally stirring, until the onion is tender and translucent, about 15 minutes.

3. Add the rice, tomato paste, fresh tomatoes, and broth. Increase the heat to high, bringing the mixture to a boil for 1 minute.

4. Reduce the heat to low, add the bell pepper and string beans, stir a few times to mix well, cover, and simmer until all the liquid is absorbed, about 20 minutes.

5. Spoon out the cooked rice onto a serving dish, and garnish with the egg slices. Serve warm.

Lasagna

One of the more memorably embarrassing moments of my teen years happened when I somehow ate an entire pan of lasagna that was meant to feed five or six hungry adults. Even though a stack of plates was sitting right next to the baking pan, I had it in my mind that this was just my portion and that somewhere—apparently hidden from my view—there were five or six other pans for my coworkers.

All these years later, I still haven't decided what the worst part of this incident was: the moment when everyone else learned that there was nothing for them to eat or when, a few minutes later, I realized that despite eating six portions of lasagna, I was both still hungry and the skinniest person there. (I was an exercise nut even back then.)

Putting this sad memory aside, lasagna is a terrific dish to make ahead for a big dinner. It lends itself to large batches, freezes well, and can be varied in ways to suit almost any diet.

Just don't eat too much of it before everybody else gets their portions.

This is a take on the classic Italian American dish.

 Lasagna with Meat Sauce
Makes 8 servings

2 tablespoons olive oil

4 anchovy fillets

2 teaspoons dried oregano

1 teaspoon dried rosemary

1 pound ground pork

1 pound ground beef

2 cups chopped onions

1 1/2 cups chopped red bell pepper

6 cloves garlic, crushed and chopped

6 cups canned crushed tomatoes or *passata* (page 20)

1 cup water

1 teaspoon salt

1 teaspoon freshly ground black pepper

Olive oil spray for the baking pan

1/2 pound uncooked lasagna pasta

1/2 cup grated Parmesan cheese

1 cup shredded mozzarella cheese

1. Heat the oil, anchovies, oregano, and rosemary in a large, heavy pan over medium heat and cook, stirring, until the anchovies break up and dissolve in the oil, about 3 minutes.

2. Add the pork and beef. Use a wooden spoon to break up the meat and make sure it doesn't clump. Cook until there are no lumps and the grains of meat are well browned with no trace of pink, about 30 minutes.

3. Mix in the onions, bell pepper, and garlic. Cook, occasionally stirring, until the onions are translucent and tender, about 30 minutes.

4. Add the tomatoes and water, and reduce the heat to medium-low. Simmer until the raw tomato taste is gone, about 20 minutes. Taste the sauce and add the salt if needed. Otherwise, add the ground pepper and set the sauce aside. Note: This mixture should be more liquid than a pasta sauce because moisture is needed to cook the pasta.

5. Preheat your oven to 400 degrees.

6. Generously spray a 9 by 13 by 2–inch baking dish with the olive oil spray. Lay out 3 sheets of the lasagna pasta on the bottom of the pan, spread a thin layer of the meat sauce over the pasta, and sprinkle some of the Parmesan cheese on top.

7. Repeat step 6 three more times so that you have four layers. Spread any remaining sauce on top, and bake for 45 minutes. At that point open the oven door and pull out the oven rack just far enough for you to safely add the shredded mozzarella and any remaining Parmesan on top, then close the oven and bake until the top begins to brown, about 20 more minutes. Allow to cool for at least 10 minutes before serving.

A vegetarian lasagna seems like something every cook should have in his or her arsenal. This one uses zucchini and eggplant, traditional Italian vegetables.

 ## Vegetable and Cheese Lasagna

Makes 8 servings

1 tablespoon olive oil

1 teaspoon dried oregano

1 teaspoon dried thyme

1 teaspoon crushed red
    pepper flakes

2 cups chopped onions

4 cloves garlic, crushed and
    chopped

6 cups canned crushed tomatoes
    or *passata* (page 20)

1 cup water

1 teaspoon salt

Olive oil spray for the baking pan

1/2 pound uncooked lasagna pasta

3 cups zucchini slices

4 cups eggplant slices

3 cups shredded mozzarella cheese

1/2 cup grated Parmesan cheese

1. Heat the oil, oregano, thyme, and red pepper flakes in a large saucepan over medium heat, and cook, stirring, until the spices are coated, about 1 minute.

2. Add the onions and garlic, and cook, occasionally stirring, until the onions are tender and translucent, about 15 minutes.

3. Mix in the tomatoes and the water. Reduce the heat to medium-low, and simmer, occasionally stirring, until the raw tomato taste is gone, about 30 minutes. Taste the sauce, and add the salt if needed. Set the sauce aside. *Note:* This mixture should have more liquid than a regular pasta sauce because moisture is needed to cook the pasta.

4. Preheat your oven to 325 degrees.

5. Generously spray a 9 by 13 by 2–inch baking dish with the olive oil spray. Lay out 3 sheets of the lasagna pasta on the bottom of the pan. Cover with a layer of zucchini and eggplant slices, spread a thin layer of the sauce on the vegetables, making sure that the pasta is covered, and sprinkle some of the mozzarella, and Parmesan cheeses on top.

6. Repeat step 5 two more times so that you have 3 layers. Spread any remaining tomato sauce and cheese on top, cover the pan (aluminum foil is fine here), and bake for 60 minutes. At that point, remove the cover, and bake until the top just begins to turn golden, about another 15 minutes. Allow to cool for at least 10 minutes before serving.

Here's a classic bean stew from a classic Caribbean island: Puerto Rico.

 ## Puerto Rican Rice and Pigeon Pea Stew (Sopa de Gandules)

Makes 4 servings

1 cup dried pigeon peas

3 cups water

2 tablespoons olive oil

2 teaspoons dried oregano

1 cup chopped red onion

3 cloves garlic, crushed and chopped

2 cups chopped fresh tomatoes

4 cups chicken broth

1/2 cup white rice

1/4 cup chopped pitted olives

2 tablespoons capers, rinsed
   and drained

1/4 cup chopped fresh cilantro

1/2 teaspoon salt

1/2 teaspoon freshly ground black pepper

1. Soak the beans in the water overnight in a bowl. Drain when you're ready to proceed with the rest of the dish.

2. Heat the oil, oregano, onion, and garlic in a heavy pot over medium heat. Cook, stirring, until the onion is tender and translucent, about 20 minutes.

3. Mix in the soaked beans, tomatoes, broth, rice, olives, and capers, and reduce the heat to medium-low. Simmer, occasionally stirring, until the beans are tender and about one-quarter of the broth has evaporated, about 45 minutes.

4. Add the cilantro, and let the mixture simmer until the cilantro is limp, about 5 minutes.

5. Taste the broth and add the salt if needed. The capers and olives may well have given it enough of a salty flavor for you, but if it needs salt, add it a pinch at a time. Then add the ground pepper and give the mixture one last good stir. Serve warm.

Is Spanish rice really Spanish? Or is it one of those Americanized dishes like chop suey or Swedish meatballs? A bit of research tells us that the recipe varies from place to place and is often associated with Mexican restaurants. This recipe will try to honor them all.

Spanish Rice
Makes 4 servings

1 tablespoon olive oil

1 teaspoon cumin powder

1/2 teaspoon chili powder

3 cloves garlic, crushed and
   chopped

1/2 cup chopped onion

1/2 cup chopped red bell pepper

1 cup chopped fresh tomatoes

1 cup long-grain white rice

2 cups chicken broth

1 teaspoon salt

1. Heat the oil, cumin, and chili in a saucepan over medium heat, and stir until the spices are dissolved in the oil.

2. Add the garlic, onion, pepper, and tomatoes, and cook, stirring, until the onion turns translucent, about 15 minutes.

3. Mix in the rice, making sure it's coated with the vegetables. Add the broth, and stir the mixture. Turn up the heat to high, and bring the mixture to a boil.

4. Let the mixture boil for 1 minute, reduce the heat to low, and simmer covered until all the liquid is absorbed, about 20 minutes. Taste the rice to check for seasonings; if needed, add the salt. Be careful here. Sometimes chicken broth will have enough salt, and sometimes it won't. You really have to taste test it. Serve warm.

Tomato Fight!

I don't believe that tomato fighting has a long or glorious history, but it sure attracts attention. The big fight in Buñol, Spain, makes the news all over the world. TV and magazine images show guys riding in the back of tomato-filled pickup trucks, throwing them at anybody they can. It looked interesting, but Spain in August seemed a bit out of reach. That's why my ears perked up when I heard about the annual Il Pomodoro Tomato Fight in Pittston, Pennsylvania. And when I saw their selling point; "You don't have to travel to Buñol, Spain, to squash and throw tomatoes at your friends and neighbors," I was there.

The fight was part of a larger tomato festival that featured a 5K run, a parade, beauty contests, concerts, and an astounding array of classic Italian American foods. Before I even got out my camera, I had eaten a bowl of pasta fagoli, eyed the bruschetta, and contemplated the ravioli. When Paul Cooper, the fight organizer told me, "You can't come to Pittston without having the tripe," I told him that I came for the fights first and foremost.

So did lots of others; a half-hour before the start, the combatants began to gather in the parking lot of Paul's restaurant, and the sound system began to belt out Louis Prima classics like "Dominic the Donkey" and "That's Amore." One teenager told me "I just got done with the run, and I heard there was a fight. . . ." There weren't just teenagers; parents, fifty-somethings, and even senior citizens were donning goggles and fight T-shirts. Waiting for them were 175 cases of rotten tomatoes—over five thousand pounds total—neatly lined up in two opposing rows.

Somehow, the crowd divided up into two reasonably even sides—individuals, teams, and even whole families (although small children had to remain on the sidelines). They then picked up handfuls of tomatoes, started squeezing them in their fists—the rules required this—and when the horn sounded, began to throw.

For a few moments, the red stuff was flying everywhere. People were screaming and cheering, and children too small to be in the melee were picking up tomatoes that had landed on the sidelines and began hurling them wherever they could. I tried to take pictures, but most of the time; my camera flashed the word "busy" in the viewfinder.

As quickly as it started, it was over. TV crews and reporters swarmed into the mob of glop-stained combatants. Many participants were rolling on the tomato-covered pavement; all were psyched. It took a few more moments for things to calm down, and then a bulldozer came out, scraped the tomato remains into a dumpster, and all that was left was the scent of tomato in the air. If you'd just stumbled upon the scene, you'd have thought that nothing more vigorous than a farmers' market had just been held there.

Isn't tomato supposed to go on *top* of the pasta? Not always. Pasta chefs often replace cooking water with juices or extracts for added flavor and visual effect. Serve this pasta with a bit of butter or olive oil and some grated Parmesan cheese.

You'll need a pasta machine for this recipe.

 Tomato Pasta

Makes 4 servings

3 cups flour plus extra for
    kneading
1 cup tomato juice
2 tablespoons olive oil
6 quarts water
2 tablespoons salt
    for cooking water

1. Combine the 3 cups of flour and tomato juice in a large bowl, and mix until no lumps remain and a dough begins to form.

2. Sprinkle some additional flour on a countertop or other flat work surface and begin kneading the dough. Knead for 3 minutes or until a thumb jabbed in the dough will just begin to bounce back.

3. Set your pasta machine to its widest opening. Take one-quarter of the kneaded dough and pass it through the pasta machine. Fold the resulting sheet in half and repeat the trip through the machine three more times.

4. Close the pasta machine opening by one notch, and repeat step 3 several more times. When the dough is smooth, elastic, and holds its shape, decrease the pasta machine opening another notch. Keep doing this until your pasta machine is at a number five or six setting. Regardless of what the machine calls it, I find that one notch away from the narrowest opening is best for both noodle and ravioli doughs.

5. If you're using the pasta for stuffing or lasagna (page 120), it's now ready to go. Skip to step 6 after the pasta is filled and formed. Otherwise, run it through the slicing blades of your pasta machine, and set on a drying rack for about 30 minutes. If you don't have a rack, lay it out flat on parchment paper with no edges touching, and let it dry the same amount of time.

6. Bring the water to a boil, and mix in the salt. Add the pasta, stir it once, and lower the heat to a simmer. Cook for 3 minutes or until the pasta is chewy but not mushy. Serve warm.

OK, "rice and tomatoes"—it couldn't be simpler. But simple dishes are often the hardest, aren't they? What sort of rice? Olive oil or butter? Chicken or beef broth? Canned or fresh tomatoes? You'll need a good skillet with a cover, too.

This recipe is my version, but if you disagree, the possibilities are infinite.

 ## Tomato–Brown Rice Pilaf

Makes 4 servings

1 tablespoon olive oil

1 teaspoon dried oregano

1/2 cup chopped onion

3 cloves garlic, chopped

1 cup brown basmati rice,
    rinsed and drained

1 cup coarsely chopped
    fresh tomato

3 cups chicken broth

1/2 teaspoon salt

1/2 teaspoon freshly ground
    black pepper

1. Heat the oil, oregano, onion, and garlic in a skillet over medium heat and cook, uncovered, stirring until the edges of the onion begin to brown. Add the rice and tomato, and stir it a bit more to make sure the rice is covered with the onion mixture.

2. Add the broth, raise the heat to high, and give the mixture a few more stirs. When the liquid begins to boil, reduce the heat to a simmer, and cover the pot. Cook undisturbed for 45 minutes or until all the liquid has been absorbed. Sprinkle with the salt and ground pepper, fluff with a fork, and serve warm.

6. pizza and baked goods

Pizza

"Pizza" may once have been a recipe, but today it's so big that it's more of a genre than a single food. Take the crust; it can be as thick as a loaf of French bread or as thin as a cracker. And the sauce can be simple crushed tomatoes, sweet, spicy, or not there. Cheese can be Buffalo Mozzarella from Italy, local fresh mozzarella, or something else entirely—I've even seen pizzas with shredded Cheddar, Colby, or queso blanco. Toppings also run the gamut. Classics like anchovies, oddballs like pineapple, and newfangled inventions like grilled chicken Caesar can all be found on modern pizza.

In central New Jersey where I live, pizza has been served since long before the word entered the English language. Back then, it was called "tomato pie," and if you think about it, that's what it was: crust, tomato, cheese, and spices. Sure, there are "white" pizzas that don't have tomato, but they're the exception, tomato is the rule—and plenty of people still call them "tomato pies."

The recipes here are a starting point, but you can vary them as much (or as little) as you'd like. While I'd prefer to stick with a few simple ingredients, feel free to make pineapple, tuna, and caviar pizza if that's what you want.

Yes, this is something you can easily buy—but why would you want to?

 ## Pizza Dough

*Makes dough for two
12-inch pies*

1 packet active dry yeast

1/2 teaspoon sugar

1 cup water, warmed to
　　100 degrees*

3 cups all-purpose flour plus
　　additional for kneading

1 teaspoon salt

Cooking oil spray

*Filtered or bottled water
works best.

1. Sprinkle the yeast and sugar into the warm water and give it a couple of stirs. Make sure there are no dry lumps. Let the mixture stand for about 10 minutes. At that point, a layer of foam should be forming at the top. This shows that the yeast is active.

2. Combine the yeast liquid with the flour and salt in a large bowl and mix until a dough begins to form. If it's too dry, add water—a tablespoon at a time—until it's soft and flexible. If it's too sticky, add flour—again, a tablespoon at a time— until it's smooth and malleable. Knead the dough on a floured countertop for 5 minutes or until the dough bounces back when you press on it with your thumb. Put the kneaded dough in a large bowl that's been coated with cooking oil, cover it (a towel is fine here), and leave it undisturbed for at least 3 hours. It should have doubled in size by then.

3. Knead the dough again for a few seconds to get the air out. Cover, and let it stand again for 2 more hours. At that point the dough will have risen a bit more. It's now ready to use.

Real Pizza—Or Just How Real Can a Pizza Be?

Pizza was the first savory food I spent my own money on—20¢ slices at the Pizza Den in Forest Hills, Queens—and the staple that sustained me throughout much of my life in both New York and Italy. Michael Pollan tells us that Mexicans think of themselves as "corn walking." I guess that makes me "pizza walking"—a six-foot-tall, stooped, potbellied, tomato-and-cheese-topped pie.

Were those slices "real" pizza? Sure . . . well, maybe not so "sure." An Italian might have to study it for a few minutes to see the connections, but for somebody raised in New York City, it was as real as real could be. Slices were my definition of pizza for decades. Later on, I learned about "New Haven Pizza" and "California Pizza," and when I married an Italian, I ate even more variations of that legendary food.

Over time, I realized that pizza was a genre, not a recipe. Slices on a Queens street, oval pies in New Haven, pies topped with caviar in Los Angeles, pies with slices of potato instead of dough, and whatever went by the name in Italy, France, Turkey, India, or right here in the U.S.A.

Pizza fanatics from the big city told me about a place on the Lower East Side. I was assured that this was "it"—fun, authentic, and delicious. The fun began almost as soon as my wife and I walked through the door. The menu—with 12-inch personal pies for $21 and cans of soda for $3 more—made us laugh. We were laughing even harder after we left (without buying anything, needless to say) and asking questions like, "Is this what pizza was intended to be?"

My first real stop on the pizza trail was Naples 45, a huge place in midtown Manhattan that was legendary for the accuracy and authenticity of its pizzas. A conversation with Chef Chris DeLuna and Head Pizzaiolo Charlie Restivo pretty much set the scene. For them, pizza was a simple and totally unforgiving food. Charlie was particularly intense; here's a guy who could be heading a major restaurant or hotel feeding operation instead of focusing on pizza. His title, Head Pizzaiolo, might mean just "head guy who makes pizza," but it also carries much more powerful implications—it says "this guy's whole life is pizza and nothing else." This is "pizza walking" redefined.

With brainpower like this, Naples 45 doesn't miss a detail. As Charlie stoked a wood-burning oven, I asked him about wood vs. coal for pizza ovens. "Coal can give a sulfur flavor," he shot back before acknowledging that in Italy, firewood is far more expensive than coal and that people in poor communities might have to use coal to keep their restaurants open at all.

A question about leavening was answered with the same intensity: ten minutes of discourse on sourdough and fresh yeast. Nothing slipped past these guys—the change in San Marzano tomatoes, the type of curd used to make their fresh mozzarella, even the water (they bring in bottled that simulates the stuff in Naples). If there was a Ph.D. in pizza science, Charlie would be the first to be awarded one.

When it was time to head into the kitchen, there was no dough in the air, just a cook with some very basic ingredients and a wood-burning oven. Charlie didn't just throw the pie in, though. Using a long-handled peel, he held the pie over the fire for a few seconds to get some color on the crust edges. The result was pale to the eyes of most Americans but perfect by Italian standards. No char (that makes it bitter), no deep brown cheese, no dried bits of tomato sauce. A trip to Italy on a plate.

Pizza Margharita is the basic. With red sauce, white cheese, and green basil leaves, it echoes the colors of the Italian flag.

For this recipe, you'll also need a pizza stone and peel (a sort of giant, long-handled spatula).

Pizza Margharita

Makes one 12-inch pie

1/2 recipe pizza dough (page 134)
1 cup canned crushed tomatoes
    or *passata* (page 20)
1/2 teaspoon salt
1/2 teaspoon freshly ground
    black pepper
1 teaspoon dried oregano
4 ounces mozzarella cheese,
    sliced thinly
2 fresh basil leaves
2 tablespoons ground cornmeal
Flour for the work surface
    and the peel

1. Place your pizza stone in a cold oven, and then preheat the oven to 550 degrees. Do NOT put a cold stone in a hot oven—it's likely to crack. The stone needs 1 hour to heat fully.

2. Sprinkle some flour on your countertop, and roll the dough out flat. (The flour will help make sure that the dough doesn't stick.) Some people use their hands, but you might find it easier to use a rolling pin. Toss a bit of flour onto your pizza peel, and then spread out the dough onto it, forming a round or oval pizza pie shape. Quickly, evenly spoon the crushed tomatoes over the dough, forming a layer. Then sprinkle the tomatoes with the salt, ground pepper, and oregano. Place the mozzarella slices evenly over the sauce. Finally, lay a basil leaf or two on top of the assembled pie.

3. Sprinkle the cornmeal on the hot pizza stone, and slide the pie off the peel and onto the stone.

4. Bake for 7 to 9 minutes. Watch the pie carefully to make sure it doesn't burn—cooking happens fast!

5. When the pizza is done, remove it from the stone immediately. Let it cool for a few moments before cutting and serving. Don't forget to close the oven door quickly so that the stone can reheat for your next pie.

This pie is perfect for those of us who are always trying to get more vegetables into our diet.

For this recipe, you'll also need a pizza stone and peel (a sort of giant, long-handled spatula).

Pizza with Vegetables
Makes one 12-inch pie

1/2 recipe pizza dough (page 134)
1 cup crushed tomatoes or
    passata (page 20)
1 teaspoon salt
1/2 teaspoon freshly ground black pepper
1/2 teaspoon dried oregano
1/2 teaspoon dried thyme
1/2 cup sliced eggplant
1/2 cup sliced zucchini
1/2 cup red bell pepper strips
4 ounces sliced mozzarella cheese
2 tablespoons ground cornmeal
2 fresh basil leaves
Flour for the work surface and the peel

1. Place your pizza stone in a cold oven, and then preheat the oven to 550 degrees. Do NOT put a cold stone in a hot oven—it's likely to crack. The stone needs 1 hour to heat fully.

2. Sprinkle some flour on your countertop, and then roll the dough out flat. (The flour will help make sure that the dough doesn't stick.) Some people use their hands, but you might find it easier to use a rolling pin. Toss a bit of flour on your pizza peel and then spread out the dough onto it. Quickly spoon the crushed tomatoes evenly over the dough, forming a layer. Then sprinkle the tomatoes with the salt, ground pepper, oregano, and thyme. Place the eggplant and zucchini slices and the pepper strips over the sauce.

3. Sprinkle the cornmeal on the hot pizza stone, and slide the pie off the peel and onto the stone.

4. Bake for 6 to 7 minutes. Watch the pie carefully to make sure it doesn't burn—cooking happens fast!

5. Slide the rack out just far enough to be able to carefully place the mozzarella slices evenly over the sauce. Finally, lay a basil leaf or two on top of the assembled pie, and bake for 4 more minutes. This step ensures that the vegetables cook through and the cheese doesn't burn.

6. When the pizza is done, remove it from the stone immediately. Let it cool for a few moments before cutting and serving. Don't forget to close the oven door quickly so that the stone can reheat for your next pie.

Variation: Leave off the cheese to make a vegan pizza. Bake the pie for 10 minutes or until the vegetables begin to brown.

No, no, no, no! These aren't instructions for warming up those frozen pizzas you buy in the supermarket. Instead, you're going to learn how to make pizzas that you can freeze and easily reheat. Note that for this recipe you'll also need a pizza stone and peel. You'll also need some gallon-size resealable freezer bags. While this size pizza works well for me, you can also make smaller pies for children or parties.

 ## Frozen Pizza
Makes 4 frozen pizzas

1 recipe pizza dough
   (page 134)*
Flour for the work
   surface and peal
3 cups canned crushed
   tomatoes or *passata*
   (page 20), divided
   into quarters
2 cups shredded
   mozzarella cheese,
   divided into quarters
2 tablespoons dried

oregano, divided
   into quarters
1 tablespoon crushed
   red pepper flakes,
   divided into quarters
1/4 cup cornmeal
*OK, if you want to, use
the store-bought stuff.
It's still better than paying somebody to drive
a pizza to your house in
the middle of the night.

1. Place your pizza stone in the cold oven, and preheat to 550 degrees. Do NOT put a cold stone in a hot oven—it's likely to crack. The stone needs 1 hour to heat fully and 10 minutes or so between pies to get back to temperature.

2. Take a piece of dough about the size of a baseball and roll it out into a 12-inch disk on a well-floured countertop. (The flour will help to make sure that the dough doesn't stick.) I use a rolling pin, but if you prefer to toss it in the air and spin it on your fingertips, do so. Try to get the dough to be just small enough to fit in a freezer bag.

3. Flour your pizza peel and lay the dough out on it.

4. Spread about one-quarter of the crushed tomatoes onto the dough in a thin, even layer. Then sprinkle with one-quarter of the mozzarella, one-quarter of the oregano, and one-quarter of the pepper flakes.

5. Dust the pizza stone with cornmeal. If the stone is hot enough, it will start smoking within seconds. Slide the pizza off the peal and onto the stone. Bake for 8 minutes or until the crust is nicely browned but not charred. Remove from the oven and let cool.

6. Repeat steps 2 through 5 three more times.

7. When the pizzas have cooled to room temperature, place in individual sealed freezer bags and put them as far back in the freezer as you can (the back of the freezer is the coldest part).

8. To reheat, preheat your oven to 450 degrees and put the frozen pizza right on the top rack. If you start with a cold oven, the pizza will take about 15 minutes to reheat; if the oven is already hot, your pizza will be ready in 9 minutes.

Variations: Any topping you put on a fresh pizza will work equally well on these frozen ones. Make sure they're all cooked together, though; don't just throw the toppings on afterward.

Lots of places that make pizza also make calzones. This isn't really a surprise; they use the same ingredients and methods, but instead of a big flat thing, you wind up with something that's a bit different: a sort of filled pie.

Note that for this recipe, you'll also need a pizza stone and peel (a sort of giant, long-handled spatula).

🌿 Tomato Calzone
Makes 4 calzones

2 tablespoons
  all-purpose flour
1 recipe pizza dough
  (page 134)
1 1/2 cups canned
  crushed tomato or
  passata (page 20),
  halved
1 cup shredded
  mozzarella
  cheese, divided
  into quarters

1/4 cup grated
  Parmesan cheese,
  divided into
  quarters
2 teaspoons dried
  oregano, divided
  into quarters
2 cups chopped, fresh
  tomatoes, divided
  into quarters
Cornmeal for the
  pizza stone

1. Place your pizza stone in the cold oven, and preheat to 550 degrees. Do NOT put a cold stone in a hot oven—it's likely to crack. The stone needs 1 hour to heat fully.

2. Dust a countertop with the flour, and roll out one-quarter of the pizza dough into a 12-inch disk. (The flour will help make sure that the dough doesn't stick.)

2. Spread one-quarter of the crushed tomatoes on top of the dough, leaving about a 1/2-inch dry edge.

3. Sprinkle one-quarter each of the mozzarella, Parmesan, oregano, and chopped tomatoes on half of the crushed tomatoes and dough.

4. Fold the half of the dough without the

toppings over the half that has them and seal the edges. Poke a few holes in the dough to make sure it doesn't burst.

5. Repeat steps 2 through 4 until you've got a full batch.

6. Dust your hot pizza stone with cornmeal and place the sealed dough packages on it. Bake at 550 degrees for 7 minutes or until the crusts are golden-brown and the edges are very crisp. Let cool 5 to 10 minutes before serving.

Think of this as a loaf of bread with a surprise inside. The bread makes a great side for savory dishes, especially those with Mediterranean flavors.

 ## Dried-Tomato and Olive Bread

Makes 2 loaves

2 cups plus 1 cup water

1 packet active dry yeast

1 teaspoon sugar

1/4 cup olive oil plus extra oil
    or oil spray for the bowl
    and baking pan

7 cups all-purpose flour plus
    extra for kneading

2 cups chopped oven-dried
    tomatoes (page 25)

1 cup chopped olives, drained

2 tablespoons dried rosemary

2 teaspoons salt

1. Heat 1 cup of the water to 100 degrees (use a thermometer to check), remove from the heat, and add the active dry yeast and sugar. Stir until the sugar is dissolved. Let the mixture stand until it begins to bubble, about 10 minutes.

2. Combine the yeast mixture, olive oil, flour, tomatoes, olives, rosemary, and salt in a large bowl along with the remaining 2 cups of water. Mix until a dough starts to form. If it's too dry, add water, 1 tablespoon at a time, until you have something sticky but not liquidy. If it's too wet, add flour, again 1 tablespoon at a time, until it's no longer gloppy.

3. Sprinkle some flour on a flat work surface, put the dough on it, and knead. The dough will become elastic after about 5 minutes. Let it rest for 2 minutes; then knead until it gets even bouncier, about 3 more minutes.

4. Oil the inside of a large bowl and place the kneaded dough at the bottom. Cover with a towel, and leave it where it won't be disturbed until it doubles in size, about 3 hours.

5. Press down on the dough so that it returns to something close to its original size (this is called "punching down" in baker's jargon), divide it in half, and shape each piece into a loaf. Put the loaves on a well-oiled baking sheet, cover with a towel, set aside in a quiet place, and let them rise one more time, about 1 hour.

6. Preheat your oven to 400 degrees.

7. Bake until the crust is golden-brown and a meat thermometer inserted in the dough reads about 200 degrees, about 45 minutes. Remove from the oven and let cool.

When the Albanians came to my house (see page 152), this is what we made:

🌿 Albanian Tomato-and-Onion Pie (Burek)

Makes 1 pie

2 tablespoons olive oil plus
    extra or cooking oil spray
    for layering the dough
1/2 teaspoon oregano
2 cups sliced onions
1/2 teaspoon salt
2 tablespoons water
2 cups thinly sliced tomatoes
1 package phyllo dough

1. Heat the olive oil, oregano, onions, and salt in a frying pan over medium-low heat and cook, stirring, until the onions are soft, about 15 minutes. Then add the water, cover the pot, and simmer until the onions are very limp, another 10 minutes.

2. Mix in the tomato slices, and cook uncovered, occasionally stirring, until the tomatoes are as limp as the onions, about 15 minutes. Set aside.

3. Preheat the oven to 375 degrees.

4. Oil a 9 by 13–inch baking dish. Arrange 4 to 6 sheets of phyllo dough so they cover the bottom of the baking dish. When laying them out, sprinkle (or spray) some oil between the sheets. Then spread half the tomato mixture on top of the layers, and cover with 4 to 6 more sheets of dough. Layer the remaining tomato mixture and top with more phyllo.

4. Bake for 40 minutes or until the top is golden brown. Let cool for 10 minutes before serving.

"Tomato pie" means different things in different places. Some people imagine an apple pie, but one filled with tomatoes (and we have that, see below); others know the phrase "tomato pie" as an archaic word for "pizza"—although in Trenton, New Jersey, it's not archaic at all. But there's also the possibility of a savory pie with tomatoes inside.

❧ Savory Tomato Pie
Makes 1 pie

1 piecrust dough, top
and bottom*
6 cups chopped fresh
tomatoes
1 cup chopped red onion
1 cup chopped yellow
bell pepper
1/2 cup dried bread-
crumbs
1 teaspoon salt
1/2 teaspoon freshly
ground black pepper
1 teaspoon dried oregano

1 cup shredded
Cheddar cheese
1/4 cup grated
Parmesan cheese
Oil or cooking oil spray
for the pie pan
*If you use a store-
bought crust, get the
kind that's folded and
refrigerated, not those
that are pressed into foil
pans and frozen.

1. Preheat the oven to 325 degrees.

2. Oil or spray a pie pan and line it with the bottom piecrust dough.

3. Mix the tomatoes, onion, bell pepper, breadcrumbs, salt, pepper, oregano, Cheddar, and Parmesan in a large bowl, making sure all the ingredients are well distributed. Pour the mixture into the pie pan. Lay the top crust over the filling, pinch the edges to seal, and use a fork to poke some holes into the top so that steam can escape.

4. Bake until the top crust is well browned, about 1 hour. Let cool before serving.

The Chefs: Albanian Invasion

It didn't take long before the lone Albanian who worked in my wife's office found out that I was testing recipes from her home country. Late in the evening I'd get hints like, "Her husband is an expert on pickled tomatoes" or "She knows how to make phyllo dough from scratch." Pretty soon it was decided: an Albanian family was going to come to our house, judge my marinated tomatoes, and teach us how to make a tomato pie.

Before this, my only knowledge of Albania came from shortwave radio broadcasts I listened to back in my teens and a couple of magazine covers I'd spotted either in Italy or the Bronx. I knew better than to expect anything that resembled either.

Soon Sonila, her daughter, Jona, and her husband, Parid, were sitting in my kitchen. The table was cleared, the ingredients were laid out, and within moments the office gossip machine was in full swing. When they weren't discussing cubicle movements or benefit choices, we somehow collectively managed to bake a *burek*—a tomato-and-onion pie with a phyllo crust (see page 150).

A cooking demonstration from a cuisine you've never tried is always an eye-opener. Maybe you've done something in a specific way your entire life and never saw it challenged—and then out of nowhere, a whole new set of rules appears. Sonila kept acting like everything she did was so obvious that it needed no explanation, and I kept being surprised. Onions had water added and were cooked covered so they became mushy. Tomatoes were added to the frying pan sliced and then sweated out so they didn't retain their shape. Somehow, it was all delicious in the end.

At dinner, I served two versions of my Albanian-Style Marinated Green Tomatoes (page 30), Eggplant Stuffed with Tomatoes (page 164), the *Burek* (page 150), and several other pies that Sonila brought. Parid was astounded that a middle-aged, male, nonchef, non-Albanian could cook so well. To preserve the yin and yang of the moment, my wife complained a bit and balanced things off.

The funniest moment? When I served the Albanian-Style Marinated Green Tomatoes (the exact batch that's in the photos), they exclaimed, "These are delicious, but why did you put cinnamon in them? We never do that." Well . . . in my book research on Albanian food, it was always listed as an ingredient. I figured we must have had an Albanian cookbook somewhere in the house—we have thousands of cookbooks—so I scoured the shelves and turned one up. Sonila anxiously thumbed to the marinated tomato recipe (one of the nation's most popular dishes.), and sure enough, it had cinnamon. After some heavy discussion, it was decided that the recipe must be from another part of Albania. And suddenly the notion of *another* regional cuisine entered my universe.

7. vegetables

I am certain that there are at least a million varieties of beans in the world and that every one of them is available in at least one small store somewhere. If you're up for this sort of search, head over to a Greek market and pick up a package of those big butter beans they call *gigantes*; otherwise, go to the dried-bean aisle of your supermarket and look for *hàbas grandes* or large lima beans. Note that canned versions of the exact same beans will also read "butter beans." Any and all of those will work for this dish.

🌿 Greek-Style Butter Beans in Tomato Sauce (Gigantes)

Makes 4 servings.

2 cups dried large
    butter or lima beans
2 tablespoons olive oil
1 cup chopped onion
4 cloves garlic, crushed
1 cup canned crushed
    tomatoes or
    passata (page 20)

2 tablespoons
    chopped parsley,
    divided
1 teaspoon salt
1/2 teaspoon freshly
    ground black
    pepper
2 cups water

1. Soak the dried beans in a large bowl filled with water for at least 12 hours. Initially the water should be twice as deep as the beans. The beans will expand and absorb the water as they soak. Drain and set aside.

2. Heat the oil, onion, and garlic in a pot over medium heat and cook, stirring, until the onion begins to turn golden at the edges.

3. Add the tomatoes, one half of the parsley, the soaked beans, salt, and pepper, and the water. Reduce the heat to medium-low and cook, occasionally stirring, for 90 minutes or until the sauce has thickened and the beans are tender. Garnish with the remaining parsley and serve.

So many people know the name of this dish, but hardly anybody outside of the Deep South can actually describe it. In fact, when you search the Internet, you come up with a movie before a menu or a recipe. But this really is a classic of Southern cooking—and even if you didn't see the film and are surprised by how they're made, they're worth a try.

You should also note that this recipe calls for "green" tomatoes in the unripe sense, not for a high-end heirloom that happens to be green.

 ## Fried Green Tomatoes

Makes 4 servings

2 cups cracker meal

1 teaspoon salt

1/2 teaspoon freshly ground
    black pepper

1/2 teaspoon chili powder

4 green tomatoes, cut into
    1/4-inch-thick slices

3 tablespoons bacon fat
    or vegetable oil

1. Combine the cracker meal (just grind up some saltines if you can't find it), salt, ground pepper, and chili powder. Make sure they're well blended.

2. Dredge the tomato slices in the cracker meal mixture. The liquid in the tomato should help the mixture stick.

3. Heat the bacon fat in a heavy skillet over medium-high heat, and fry the tomato slices until the cracker meal mixture becomes well browned. Flip the slices with a spatula and cook the other side. Make sure both sides are evenly cooked, about 4 minutes per side. Serve immediately—like most fried foods, fried green tomatoes don't take well to sitting or reheating.

This recipe is great when you have ripe tomatoes at the peak of the season. But it also does a fine job of concentrating flavors when you have tomatoes of less-than-stellar quality.

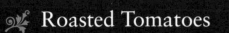

Roasted Tomatoes

Makes 4 servings

1/4 cup olive oil

4 large ripe tomatoes, cut in half

1 teaspoon dried oregano

1 teaspoon salt

1/2 teaspoon freshly ground
   black pepper

1. Preheat the oven to 325 degrees.

2. Lightly coat a cookie sheet with some of the olive oil, and place the tomato halves on it cut sides up.

3. Sprinkle the tomatoes with the oregano, salt, and pepper, and then brush with the remainder of the olive oil.

4. Bake for 45 minutes or until the tops of the tomatoes begin to brown. Serve warm.

The Tomato Farmers: Mingodale Farm

Even before you get to Mingodale Farm, you notice just how unspoiled the area is. It's miles from a convenience store—and even farther from those big-box places. Yet Mingodale Farm is in Baltimore County, Maryland, home to a large and vibrant city.

When you talk to John Foster, one of the two partners who farm here, you start to wonder which came first, this farm—on land granted by Lord Baltimore during colonial days—or the big city that's down the road a bit. John's been farming on this property all his life and tells me that at least six generations of his ancestors did the same.

Mingodale Farm hasn't always specialized in growing fancy tomatoes. Its 70 very hilly acres are perfect for grazing, and for most of John's life and generations before him, it was a dairy farm, selling milk to the local co-op until his father passed away in 1982. After that, John realized that "agriculture had two faces, large and small," and he needed to become the best sort of small specialty producer to survive.

John's partner, Hope Pezzulla, has a different story. Years spent as a Baltimore paralegal and a lifetime of dreams inspired by *Little House on the Prairie* caused her to make the move from gardener to farmer and from city to country. Yes . . . Hope is a real romantic, and her farming dreams are still vivid after four years of working the soil. "I wanted to create a community-type farm," she says, "not just come in and buy and leave. People can come in and talk and bring their coffee."

As Hope and John showed me a flat of heirlooms—which were

quickly covered with condensation as if they had come out of a fridge on that hot August day—their pride and excitement were like electricity in the air. There were San Marzanos, Big Beefs, Celebrities, Striped Germans, and Brandywines. John also spoke of Mr. Stripys and Great Whites as he arranged them into still lifes for me to photograph. I reciprocated by setting up my lights and giving it my all.

When asked about their favorite ways to eat tomatoes, John's answer was quick: "A slice on top of a burger." Hope answered, "Stewed with oregano and parsley." Then together in a chorus, "Fried green tomatoes!"

I couldn't agree more. I also agree that—with the rolling hills, grazing cows, and those tomatoes—this may well be the place where Hope's Little House dreams are realized. Head on over to Mingodale Farm, bring your coffee, and decide for yourself.

Believe it or not, some of us are old enough to remember when ratatouille was a really exotic dish, and the idea of a French recipe that didn't have lots of butter, animal fat, and difficult technique was a bit much for many of us to accept.

During the cooking, a question kept running through my mind: "If this is just supposed to be glop, how did it become a French classic?" Several potfuls later, the answer appeared: With the right cooking technique, you can get bright flavors and good texture. Traditional recipes call for cooking each vegetable separately; however, I wanted a one-pot method that delivers something worthy of the ingredients going in it.

 French Vegetable Stew (Ratatouille)

Makes 4 servings

2 tablespoons olive oil

1 three-inch sprig
    fresh rosemary

1 1/2 teaspoons
    fresh thyme

1 bay leaf

2 cups sliced onions

8 cloves garlic, coarsely
    chopped

2 cups coarsely chopped
    red and/or yellow
    bell peppers

2 cups cubed eggplant

2 cups sliced zucchini

2 cups coarsely chopped
    tomatoes

2 tablespoons chopped
    fresh basil leaves

1 teaspoon salt

1/2 teaspoon freshly
    ground black pepper

1. Heat the oil, rosemary, thyme, and bay leaf in a large skillet or sauté pan* over medium heat and cook, stirring, until the herbs are coated with the oil, about 1 minute.

2. Add the onions, cooking, occasionally stirring, until they're translucent, about 5 minutes. Reduce the heat to medium-low and stir in the garlic. Cook the mixture until the onions are limp and beginning to brown at the edges, another 15 minutes.

3. Mix in the bell peppers and cook, occasionally stirring, until the peppers are tender, about 15 minutes.

4. Add the eggplant, zucchini, and tomatoes. Cook until the eggplant is tender and the liquid in the pot has reduced to a thick sauce, about 45 minutes.

5. Remove the rosemary sprig, mix in the basil leaves, salt, and pepper, and give it a few stirs to distribute well. Serve warm.

*Resist the temptation to cook ratatouille in a stock or pasta pot. This is most often the reason for gloppy, souplike ratatouille—something you want to avoid at all costs. Instead, use a skillet or large frying pan. This gives you a shallow layer of vegetables spread out over a large area. More of it will brown rather than steam. It makes a big difference.

Tomato sauce shows up in curry recipes, but it's not often that tomatoes themselves become the centerpiece. Serve this dish with rice and tomato chutney (page 202).

 ## Curried Tomatoes
Makes 4 servings

2 tablespoons butter or ghee

1 teaspoon mustard powder

2 teaspoons chili powder

1/2 teaspoon turmeric

1 teaspoon garam
   masala powder

1 teaspoon salt

2 cups chopped onions

6 cups coarsely chopped
   tomatoes

1 cup green peas

1. Warm the butter or ghee in a saucepan over medium heat, and mix in the mustard, chili, turmeric, garam masala, and salt. Cook, stirring, until the spices are coated with oil and give off a strong fragrance, about 1 minute.

2. Add the onions and reduce the heat to medium-low, stirring occasionally, until the onions are tender and translucent, about 40 minutes. Don't try to speed things up by raising the heat; you'll just scorch the mixture.

3. Add the tomatoes and peas and cook until the tomatoes are tender, the liquid has partially evaporated, and you have a thick sauce, about 45 minutes. Serve hot.

Yes, *Imam Bayildi* means "The Imam fainted." But why? Answers vary. Some say it was the very deliciousness of the meal; others claim it was the amount he ate. Another theory is that he fainted when he heard how much oil was in it. My vote is that the sheer volume of garlic did him in. That means it's a perfect dish for garlic lovers, then, doesn't it?

I prefer serving this dish as a warm appetizer, but many authorities on Turkish food suggest that it be eaten cold. The choice is yours.

 ## Eggplant Stuffed with Tomatoes (Imam Bayildi)

Makes 4 servings

2 medium eggplants
4 tablespoons
   olive oil, divided
1 teaspoon salt, divided
1 teaspoon freshly ground
   black pepper, divided
1 teaspoon sugar
2 tablespoons lemon juice
2 cups chopped onions
8 cloves garlic, chopped
2 cups chopped
   fresh tomatoes

1. Preheat the oven to 325 degrees.

2. Cut the stems off the eggplants, and trim a bit off one side so that they can sit open-face up without rolling over. Finally, use a melon baller or grapefruit spoon to form a hollow cavity in each piece.

3. Brush the trimmed eggplants with 2 tablespoons of the olive oil, and then sprinkle them with 1/2 teaspoon of the salt, 1/2 teaspoon of the pepper, sugar, and lemon juice. Place them on an oiled baking sheet.

4. Combine the remaining 2 tablespoons of oil, 1/2 teaspoon of salt, and 1/2 teaspoon of pepper in a skillet over medium heat, and then add the onions and garlic. Cook, stirring, until the onions are tender, about 10 minutes.

5. Add the tomatoes, and reduce the heat to medium-low. Simmer uncovered until the tomatoes become tender and the liquid thickens, about 20 minutes.

6. Fill the cavities in the eggplants with the tomato mixture and bake until much of the liquid has evaporated and the eggplant is very tender, about 45 minutes.

Here's a baked tomato dish with nothing but vegetables, a bit of butter, and some breadcrumbs.

 ## Chopped Tomato Casserole

Makes 4 servings

6 cups chopped fresh tomatoes

1 teaspoon salt

1/2 teaspoon freshly ground
    black pepper

1/2 teaspoon dried oregano

1 cup chopped onion

1 cup chopped celery

1/4 cup melted butter for
    the topping plus extra
    for the baking dish

1 cup unseasoned, dried
    breadcrumbs

1. Preheat the oven to 325 degrees.

2. Combine the tomatoes, salt, pepper, oregano, onion, and celery in a large bowl, and mix until everything is well combined. Then grease a 10-inch baking dish with butter and pour the tomato mixture into it.

3. Mix the melted butter and breadcrumbs together. Make sure that all the bread is moist and that there are no lumps. Spread this paste on top of the tomato mixture to form a crust.

4. Bake for 2 hours or until the crust is golden-brown and the tomato mixture is bubbling. Let it cool for 15 minutes before serving.

Southern New Jersey isn't just south of New York and Philadelphia—it's far enough down there to have recipes that strongly resemble dishes from Alabama or Georgia. With a milk-and-flour gravy, this one has obvious roots.

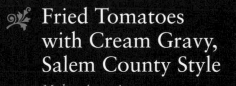

Fried Tomatoes with Cream Gravy, Salem County Style

Makes 4 servings

1 cup all-purpose flour

1 teaspoon salt

1/2 teaspoon freshly ground
   black pepper

4 cups tomato slices,
   3/8-inch thick

1/4 cup peanut oil, divided

1 cup chopped tomatoes

1 1/2 cups milk

1. Combine the flour, salt, and ground pepper. Make sure they're well mixed.

2. Dredge the tomato slices in the flour mixture. They should be evenly coated. Reserve the leftover flour.

3. Heat half the oil in a heavy skillet over medium-high heat, and fry the floured tomato slices until they're golden-brown on both sides. Unless you have a really big pan, this will go best in small batches. When the tomatoes are all fried, wipe the pan clean.

4. Lower the heat to medium, and add the remaining oil and chopped tomatoes. Cook, stirring, until the tomatoes are tender. Then sprinkle in 2 tablespoons of the reserved flour, and stir until it's absorbed by the oil and tomato.

5. With continuous stirring, add the milk a bit at a time until you have a thick gravy.

6. Arrange the tomato slices on a serving plate, and pour the warm gravy over them. Serve immediately.

If you're thinking of making something like an apple pie but filled with tomatoes, you'll have to make Savory Tomato Pie (page 151). This is something else: a baked casserole of tomatoes and cheese. Like pizza without the crust.

Tomato and Mozzarella Casserole

Makes 6 servings

2 tablespoons olive oil

1/2 cup unseasoned,
    dry breadcrumbs

5 cups tomato slices

1 teaspoon dried oregano

1/2 teaspoon salt

1/2 teaspoon freshly ground
    black pepper

1 cup shredded mozzarella
    cheese

2 tablespoons chopped parsley

1. Preheat the oven to 375 degrees.

2. Brush the inside of a baking dish with the oil. Coat the bottom with about one-quarter of the breadcrumbs and a layer of the tomato slices. Sprinkle each layer with a bit of the oregano, some more breadcrumbs, some of the salt, pepper, and some shredded cheese, reserving a bit of the breadcrumbs and cheese for garnish. When the layering is complete, bake for 45 minutes or until the tomatoes begin to brown. Remove from the oven.

3. Sprinkle the casserole with the chopped parsley and the remaining cheese and breadcrumbs in an even layer over the tomatoes. Return to the oven for 30 minutes.

4. When done, let the casserole cool for at least 15 minutes before serving.

This is one of those recipes that has so many variations, they could almost fill a book. Of course, each creator insists that he or she has the original and authentic version and everybody else's is just plain wrong.

❧ Sicilian Vegetable Stew (Caponata)

Makes 4 servings

3 tablespoons olive oil

1 teaspoon dried oregano

3 cups fresh eggplant, cut into 1/2-inch cubes

4 cloves garlic, chopped

2 tablespoons capers, rinsed and drained

1/2 cup chopped olives

1 cup chopped onion

1 cup canned crushed tomatoes or *passata* (page 20)

1/4 cup red wine vinegar

1 tablespoon sugar

1/4 cup raisins

1/4 cup pine nuts

1/2 teaspoon salt

1/4 teaspoon freshly ground black pepper

1/2 cup water

1. Heat the oil and oregano in a skillet over medium-high heat, and fry the eggplant until it starts to brown, about 15 minutes.

2. Add the garlic, capers, olives, and onions and cook, stirring, until the onions are translucent, about 15 minutes.

3. Mix in the tomatoes, vinegar, sugar, raisins, pine nuts, salt, pepper, and water, reduce the heat to low, and simmer, occasionally stirring, for about 20 minutes, or until the eggplant is fully cooked and the raisins are tender. Serve warm or cold.

The Vendors: The Fair Food Farm Stand

Tomato people are idealists. Theirs was one of the first crops to be vilified as they morphed from prizes of the garden to tasteless orbs as supermarket food took over America a half-century ago, and like ex-smokers, they remember the horrors of their former lives all too well. This romanticism translates into some remarkable products. Culton Organics (page 200) and the John J. Jeffries Restaurant (page 50), both in Lancaster County, Pennsylvania, are driving forces in a new movement for local foods and cooking traditions.

But neither is close enough to the big city to make a trip there easy. And since no one is going to drive 50 miles every time they want a tomato, that's where the Fair Food Farm Stand comes in. Located in the sprawling Reading Terminal Market, a favorite food shopping and dining venue in downtown Philadelphia, the stand gives those passionate idealists in the country an urban outlet for their foods.

The market isn't lacking for other things to eat, either. It has bakeries, coffee roasters, "conventional" produce stands, fish mongers, butchers, and some really great cheese and cold cuts. But although the meat and seafood guys might happen to get some nearby stuff, Fair Food is the only outfit that makes local farm produce its specialty.

The Fair Food Farm Stand was the first project of the White Dog Café Foundation. The café itself was making an effort to buy from local farmers, and the foundation wanted to do something more to bring their produce to Philadelphia. The response to the farm stand was quick and gratifying. Reading Terminal Market customers were sincerely excited to find the stand there and needless to say, they were most thrilled by the tomatoes. "I don't know why I'm doing this!" was a typical comment made while a customer was plunking down forty bucks or more on some assortment of heirloom, plum, or cherry tomatoes.

Educating customers is an important part of Fair Food's mission, and telling stories about the supplying farmers has made their lives more vivid. Hearing about the personal effort that went into a given farm or crop has helped spread the enthusiasm that the Fair Food crew feels.

Secretly, I wanted to know what each and every customer was doing with those tomatoes. But since I was being intrusive enough without bugging their customers, too, I settled for asking Sarah Cain, the stand's supervisor. "I just slice them with red onion and feta cheese, and that's my salad," she told me. "One of my old bosses—a fantastic tomato farmer— all he eats in the summer are loaves of white bread, Hellman's mayo (it has to be Hellman's), and a few slices of whatever tomatoes he's grown. And that's his lunch."

Sarah also spoke of tomato varieties. Her favorites? Heirlooms with a history in this area. "Not just Brandywines. There's a wonderful small tomato called a Red Calabash. Raphaelle Peale, the painter son of the founder of the Pennsylvania Academy of the Fine Arts, painted a draped figure holding a Red Calabash grown in the late 1700s. It's a really delicious, dense, juicy, round, slicing tomato."

Is a stop at Fair Food a substitute for a day in the country? Not really—but the Reading Terminal Market is a great day trip in itself. And during tomato season—or any season—for fresh produce fans, there's no better place to shop.

I'm always amazed at the number of different tomato-flavored dishes that seem to be perfect next to grilled foods—for example: ketchup (page 197), relish (page 199), and Heirloom Tomato Salad (page 38). Let's add Boston Baked Beans to the list. They're wonderful with hot dogs and burgers, and although they take a long time to prepare, they can be on the side soaking or simmering while you work on something else.

Boston Baked Beans

Makes 8 servings

3 cups dried pinto beans

2 cups chopped onions

6 ounces salt pork, cut
   into dice-sized cubes

1 teaspoon freshly ground
   black pepper

6 whole cloves

1 teaspoon mustard powder

1/2 cup molasses

1 cup canned crushed tomatoes
   or *passata* (page 20)

4 cups water

1. Soak the beans in 10 cups of water for at least 24 hours. Change the water every morning and evening. When you're ready to bake them, give them one last rinse, and then drain them thoroughly.

2. Preheat your oven to 325 degrees.

3. Combine the soaked beans with the onions, salt pork, ground pepper, cloves, mustard powder, molasses, tomatoes, and the 4 cups of water in a Dutch oven, and mix well.

4. Bake for 5 hours, occasionally stirring. The beans will be ready when the sauce is very thick and the onions and salt pork have pretty much melted away. Serve warm.

Variation: If you use canned navy beans instead of dried, you can skip the soaking and cut the time in the oven down to 2 hours. Will it taste as good as it does when you start with dried beans? I don't think so—but it will still be better than the precooked canned stuff.

If you eat often enough in Central African restaurants, you'll notice that tomatoes show up in both familiar and surprising roles. Here we find them with curry, coconut, and peanut butter—Asia and Africa in one pot. Serve this dish warm with plain rice or Jollof Rice (page 117).

 ## Spinach and Tomato in African Curry Sauce (Mchicha)

Makes 4 Servings

2 tablespoons peanut oil

2 teaspoons curry powder

1 cup chopped onion

1 cup diced canned tomatoes

1 package (16 ounces) frozen
   spinach, thawed

3 tablespoons peanut butter

1 cup coconut milk

1/2 teaspoon salt

1. Heat the oil and curry powder in a heavy pot over medium heat, and stir until the spices are coated with the oil and become fragrant, about 1 minute.

2. Mix in the onion and tomatoes, cooking, occasionally stirring, until the onion becomes translucent, about 15 minutes.

3. Add the spinach, peanut butter, coconut milk, and salt, and cook, stirring, until the mixture is heated through and well combined, about 5 minutes.

8. sauces

They don't call this "basic" for nothing. With a bit of this sauce and some pasta, you have a meal. Pour it over roast chicken, and you've transformed it. Put a few shrimp in it, and you have a seafood dish. It even works with rice or couscous.

🌿 Basic Tomato Sauce
Makes 3 cups

1 tablespoon olive oil

2 teaspoons dried oregano

1/2 teaspoon freshly ground
black pepper

2 cloves garlic, crushed and
chopped

3 cups canned crushed tomatoes
or *passata* (page 20)

1/2 teaspoon salt

1. Heat the oil in a heavy skillet over medium heat, add the oregano, ground pepper, and garlic, and cook, stirring, until the garlic turns translucent, about 4 minutes.

2. Lower the heat to medium-low. Add the tomatoes and simmer, occasionally stirring, until the flavors combine and approximately one-quarter of the liquid evaporates, about 15 minutes.

3. Taste the sauce; add the salt if needed. (Because canned tomatoes differ so much, you have to taste and test.) Serve warm or use in other recipes as called for.

Generations of comedians have made jokes about "the sauce"—that big pot of red stuff Italian American families had simmering on the stove at all times. Growing up in the New York area, I ate carloads of it and came to create my own version. It goes over pasta, of course, and roast chicken and meat loaf and potatoes and polenta, and I suspect that there are some people who just eat it with a spoon.

Sunday Gravy

Makes 6 servings

2 tablespoons olive oil

3 anchovy fillets

1/2 teaspoon chili flakes

1/4 teaspoon dried sage

1/2 teaspoons dried oregano

8 ounces ground beef

8 ounces sweet Italian sausage,
    removed from the casings

2 cups chopped onions

4 cloves garlic, crushed and chopped

3 cups canned crushed tomatoes
    or *passata* (page 20)

2 tablespoons tomato paste

1 cup chicken or beef broth

1. Heat the oil and anchovy fillets in a large pot over medium heat. Cook, stirring, until the anchovies have dissolved, about 3 minutes.

2. Mix in the chili, sage, and oregano, and cook until all the spices are covered with oil and begin to give off their fragrance, about 1 minute.

3. Add the ground beef and sausage. Use a wooden spoon to break up the meat into smaller pieces as it cooks. Keep cooking until the meat is well browned—you don't want gray here—about 20 minutes.

4. Reduce the heat to medium-low, and add the onions and garlic. Cook, occasionally stirring, until the onions are translucent, tender, and just starting to brown, about 30 minutes. (Don't try to speed this up or you'll scorch the sauce.)

5. Mix in the tomatoes, tomato paste, and broth. Give the sauce a few good stirs and let it simmer on a low burner until about one-quarter of the liquid has evaporated and the onions have just about been absorbed, about 45 minutes. Serve warm with . . . well, almost everything.

I don't know if actual wars have been fought over the ingredients that belong in this sauce, but the anger that surrounds this topic—mostly about what sort of meat is used; some say all mortadella, others ground pork, and there's even a contingent that swears by beef—leads me to conclude that the answer might be more than one. What I do in situations like this is to combine the best parts of my favorite versions. Serve over a simple pasta like spaghetti or tagliatelle.

 ## Meat Sauce for Pasta (Bolognaise)

Makes 3 cups, enough for 6 servings of pasta

1 tablespoon olive oil

3 anchovy fillets

1 teaspoon dried oregano

4 cloves garlic, crushed and chopped

1/2 cup (about 1/4 pound) chopped mortadella

1/2 cup chopped onion

1/2 pound ground pork

2 cups canned crushed tomatoes or *passata* (page 20)

1/2 teaspoon salt

1/2 teaspoon freshly ground black pepper

1. Heat the oil and anchovies in a saucepan over medium heat and cook, stirring, until the anchovies dissolve in the oil, about 3 minutes.

2. Add the oregano, garlic, and mortadella, cooking, occasionally stirring, until the garlic and mortadella begin to brown at the edges, about 8 minutes.

3. Mix in the onion and pork, and continue cooking until the pork is no longer gray and starts turning brown and the onion is translucent, about 15 minutes.

4. Add the tomatoes, salt, and ground pepper, lower the heat to a simmer, and keep cooking until the flavors combine and the raw tomato taste is gone, about 15 more minutes.

"Angry?" Well that depends on how many chilies you add. But even if you don't add any, it's still an easy sauce made with fresh tomatoes.

Serve this sauce over pasta. Penne is the traditional shape, but you can try other small shapes too. Orecchiette, "little ears," aren't exactly authentic, but they work really well here.

🦋 Pasta with "Angry" Fresh Tomato Sauce (Penne Arrabiata)

Makes sauce for 4 servings

1 tablespoon
   olive oil
1 teaspoon
   dried oregano
3 cloves garlic,
   crushed and
   chopped
1 tablespoon
   chopped fresh
   hot chili pepper*

3 cups chopped
   fresh plum
   tomatoes
1 teaspoon salt
1/2 teaspoon
   freshly ground
   black pepper
*More, if you like
the heat.

1. Heat the oil and oregano in a saucepan over high heat, and sauté until the spices are coated with oil, about 10 seconds.

2. Add the garlic and chilies, cooking them until the garlic pieces begin to brown at the edges, about 1 minute. Keep a careful eye on things to make sure the garlic doesn't burn.

3. Lower the heat to medium. Mix in the tomatoes, salt, and pepper, and simmer, occasionally stirring, until the tomato is tender and the raw flavor has gone, about 15 minutes.

On Buying Canned Tomatoes in Italy

In an American supermarket, little says "Italian" more than those big cans of tomato that often fill half an aisle. On a recent trip to Italy, I started wondering just how Italian they really were. There seemed only one way to check: Go to a large, crowded supermarket and take a look at what people were buying.

The Iper-Standa store in Borgo san Dalmazzo seemed like a perfect place to indulge in some research. It's near where my wife's relatives live, and I shop there often enough to know where most items are without asking. While the amount of shelf space taken up by canned tomato products was about the same as in New Jersey, there were many fewer varieties—just row after row of recloseable jars and Tetra Pak cartons of *passata di pomodoro*. There were jars that were on sale, jars that were always cheap, and jars with stylish labels and high prices.

Supermarket regulars in Italy will know about the huge quantities that people there typically throw in their carts. (Italians are fond of asking me why a person would ever need to buy just one roll of toilet paper.) Shrink-wrapped packages with six one-liter glass bottles of *passata* were being snapped up by everybody.

All those products on the shelf reflected just how important this one ingredient is to the local cuisine. In fact, this was in Piemonte, an area famous for *not* using much tomato. Nonetheless, local consumers always kept a bottle of *passata* in the fridge. A splash of it over a frying pan full of ground meat and garlic made a sauce for a pasta dish, another bit added to a roast in the oven transformed drippings into gravy, and just another little bit over cooking vegetables turned them into something that you could put on the table quickly.

Of course, Italian shoppers still face some of the same choices we do; there was a bewildering assortment of prepared sauces and a whole other collection of roughly the same stuff—but organic, in the "health" section on the other side of the store.

And tomato paste? They sell that in tubes. Not a giant can in sight.

This looks like Italian sauce, and it contains tomatoes and onions, but the resemblance stops there. This sauce is great over pasta, vegetables (green beans are a favorite), and even meats.

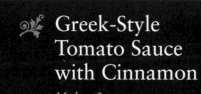

Greek-Style Tomato Sauce with Cinnamon

Makes 2 cups

2 tablespoons
   olive oil
1 teaspoon dried
   oregano
1/4 teaspoon
   ground cinnamon
1/4 teaspoon
   ground allspice
1 cup chopped onion
1 clove garlic,
   crushed and
   chopped

3 cups chopped
   fresh tomatoes
1/2 cup dry
   red wine
1 cup water
1/2 teaspoon salt
1/2 teaspoon freshly
   ground black
   pepper
1 tablespoon
   chopped
   fresh parsley

1. Heat the oil, oregano, cinnamon, and allspice in a saucepan over medium heat, and stir to make sure the spices are coated with the oil.

2. Add the onion and garlic and cook, stirring, until the onion is translucent and evenly coated with the spices, about 10 minutes.

3. Remove the saucepan from the heat, and mix in the tomatoes, wine, and water. Give the sauce a good stir, and return the pan to a medium-low burner. Simmer, occasionally stirring, until the tomatoes have broken down and the liquid has reduced by half, about 60 minutes. The sauce can be puréed at this point, but it isn't necessary.

4. Add the salt, ground pepper, and parsley, and serve immediately.

Note: If you're making this sauce ahead, don't add the parsley until you're ready to serve it.

Not every dish is what you think it is. "Tomato sauce" might mean a long-cooked purée of tomatoes and herbs like oregano and basil most of the time, but there are some big exceptions. This version from Romania can rightfully be described as "tomato sauce," but don't go looking for oregano or basil.

In Romania, this would be served over dumplings or meatballs, but it's also great with baked fish, chicken, or even pork chops.

 ## Romanian Tomato Sauce (Sos de Roşii)

Makes 2 cups

1 tablespoon vegetable oil
1 cup chopped onion
2 tablespoons tomato
    paste
1 tablespoon all-purpose
    flour
1 cup vegetable broth*
1/2 teaspoon salt
1/4 teaspoon freshly
    ground black pepper

1/2 cup white wine
*Hard-core Eastern European cooks will use *Delikat, Aromat,* or *Vegeta* instead. You'll find them in the ethnic section of your supermarket . . . sometimes.

1. Heat the oil in a heavy pot over medium heat, and sauté the onion until it begins to brown at the edges, about 10 minutes.

2. Mix in the tomato paste and cook, stirring, until it's evenly blended with the onion, about 2 minutes.

3. Mix in the flour—make sure it's completely dissolved—and then add the broth 1 tablespoon at a time until the sauce begins to thicken, about 5 minutes.

4. Add the salt, ground pepper, and wine, and simmer until the sauce thickens again, about 15 more minutes.

Here's another one of those tomato sauces that's different—but still tomato sauce. In Basque country, sauces like this one are served over everything from fish to chicken or lamb to boiled potatoes.

Basque Pepper and Tomato Sauce

Makes 3 cups

1/4 cup olive oil
1/2 teaspoon dried thyme
1 teaspoon paprika
1 bay leaf
1/2 cup chopped cooked ham
1 cup chopped onion
1/2 cup chopped red pepper
4 cloves garlic, chopped
3 cups chopped fresh tomatoes
1/2 teaspoon salt
1/4 teaspoon freshly ground
    black pepper

1. Heat the olive oil, thyme, paprika, bay leaf, and ham in a heavy pot over medium heat, and sauté until the edges of the ham pieces begin to brown, about 10 minutes.

2. Mix in the onion, red pepper, and garlic, cooking until the pepper pieces are tender and the onion translucent, about 20 minutes.

3. Add the tomatoes, salt, and ground pepper, and simmer uncovered, occasionally stirring, until one-third of the liquid has evaporated, about 30 minutes. Remove the bay leaf, set the sauce aside, and let cool.

4. Purée the sauce in a blender or food processor. There should be no lumps left. Serve warm.

So you thought you knew what tomato sauce was? Here's one more variation—uncooked, with roots in Hungary and Serbia—that expands the tomato sauce universe in another direction. Think of this as a sort of barbecue sauce, or serve it over cold meats.

Eastern European Spicy Tomato Sauce

Makes 2 cups

Combine the tomatoes, onion, salt, pepper, paprika, and oil in a blender and purée. There should be no large pieces of onion left. Store in the refrigerator.

2 cups chopped fresh tomatoes

1/2 cup chopped red onion

1/2 teaspoon salt

1/2 teaspoon freshly ground
    black pepper

1 teaspoon hot paprika

2 tablespoons olive oil

In this recipe, we use tomatoes and walnuts and the pesto ("paste") method to get a very different tomato-based pasta sauce. Serve on top of freshly cooked spaghetti or linguine.

 ## Tomato Pesto

*Makes enough for
4 servings of pasta*

1 cup sun-dried tomatoes
   (store bought or
   Oven-Dried Tomatoes,
   page 25)
1 cup extra-virgin olive oil
3 cloves garlic
1/2 cup walnuts
1/4 cup grated Parmesan
   cheese
2 tablespoons chopped
   Italian parsley
1/2 teaspoon salt
1/2 teaspoon freshly
   ground black pepper

1. Combine the tomatoes, olive oil, garlic, walnuts, grated cheese, parsley, salt, and ground pepper in a food processor, and blend into a thick paste. This might take more effort than it seems, but if you start by pulsing it a bit and then run it longer and longer as the ingredients break down, you'll get there. It's ready when no big lumps remain.

2. Store the remainder in a tightly closed container and refrigerate. The pesto will keep in the refrigerator for at least 2 weeks.

"Tomato sauce" could mean something out of a jar; something you cooked yourself for hours, like "Sunday Gravy" (page 178); something you quickly put together, like "Basic Tomato Sauce" (page 177); or a recipe like this with no cooking at all.

To serve, toss with drained, cooked pasta. It works best with larger shapes like penne and rigatoni.

 ## Raw Tomato Sauce

Makes 4 servings

2 cups chopped fresh tomatoes

1/2 cup olive oil

1 clove garlic, crushed
   and chopped

3 tablespoons chopped
   fresh basil leaves

1/2 teaspoon salt

1/2 teaspoon freshly ground
   black pepper

1. Combine the tomatoes, oil, garlic, basil, salt, and ground pepper in a large bowl, and mix well. Make sure that all the ingredients are evenly distributed.

2. Let the mixture stand for at least 30 minutes to allow the flavors to combine. Refrigerate.

"Red sauce" seems to be a euphemism for "Southern Italian," but it takes more than a bit of tomato to recreate the intense flavors of the region. This recipe—with salt cod, pine nuts, chilies, and raisins—does the job perfectly. Serve over large pasta shapes like ziti or rigatoni.

 ## Southern Italian–Style Pasta Sauce with Cod, Olives, and Raisins

Makes 4 servings

8 ounces salt cod fillets or 12 ounces fresh
   or frozen cod fillet*

2 tablespoons olive oil

3 anchovy fillets

1 teaspoon dried oregano

1/2 teaspoon chili flakes

1/2 teaspoon freshly ground black pepper

5 cloves garlic, crushed and chopped

2 tablespoons pine nuts

1 cup chopped pitted olives**

1/4 cup raisins

1 cup canned crushed tomatoes or
   passata (page 20)

*Why the difference between fresh and salted?
Salt cod is has its water removed, so it's denser.
When you use fresh, you need more but only
because the flesh contains more water.

**Please don't use canned olives here.

1. To soak the cod, first rinse it under running water to remove the surface salt. Then immerse it in a nonmetallic pan filled with water and refrigerate. Change the water every morning and evening. The fish should be soaked a minimum of two days, although I find that a third day often makes a big difference. When you're ready to cook with it, drain, pat dry, and treat it as if it were fresh fish. (While this dish works best with salt cod, if your market's fresh or frozen cod fillets look best, use them.)

2. Heat the oil and anchovies in a skillet over medium heat and cook, stirring, until the anchovies have dissolved in the oil, about 3 minutes.

3. Add the oregano, chili flakes, ground pepper, and garlic, cooking until the garlic just begins to brown at the edges, about 3 minutes.

4. Break up the soaked cod into small pieces and add to the oil mixture. Mix well, making sure that all the fish is coated. Cook, stirring, until the fish begins to turn golden, about 5 minutes.

5. Mix in the pine nuts, olives, raisins, and tomatoes, reduce the heat to medium-low, and simmer until about one-third of the liquid evaporates and a thick sauce forms, about 20 minutes. Serve warm.

9. condiments

Most ketchup recipes are for canning; they call for huge quantities of everything and all that canning equipment that most people no longer even have. This one is different, though. It's for just three cups—enough to put in the fridge for a few weeks or to make for a special occasion.

✤ Tomato Ketchup
Makes 3 cups

1 tablespoon peanut oil

1/2 teaspoon ground mace

1/2 teaspoon freshly ground
   black pepper

1/4 teaspoon ground cloves

1/4 teaspoon mustard powder

1/4 teaspoon five-spice powder

1/2 teaspoon salt

1 cup chopped onion

1 clove garlic, crushed and
   chopped

5 cups diced tomatoes

1/4 cup cider vinegar

2 tablespoons brown sugar

1. Heat the oil in a saucepan over medium-high heat, and add the mace, pepper, cloves, mustard, five-spice powder, and salt, and stir until you can smell the spices cooking, about 1 minute.

2. Reduce the heat to medium-low, and add the onion and garlic. Cook, stirring, until the onion is tender, translucent, and evenly coated with the spices, about 10 minutes.

3. Mix in the tomatoes, vinegar, and brown sugar. Simmer, occasionally stirring, until the liquid has reduced by roughly one-quarter, about 1 hour.

4. Reduce the heat further to low, to prevent scorching, and keep simmering until another one-quarter of the liquid has evaporated, about 1 more hour.

5. Turn off the heat and let the mixture cool. When it nears room temperature, purée it in a food processor, and store in the refrigerator.

"Butter" is a word that has a few other meanings besides the stuff that comes from milk. This recipe is for a sweetened fruit paste that's served like jam. You'll find apple butter almost anywhere and a wide variety of fruit butters at Amish markets. There, tomato will be mixed in along with peach, pumpkin, and pear butter.

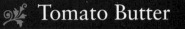

Tomato Butter

Makes 2 cups

8 cups chopped fresh tomatoes

1/2 cup sugar

1/2 cup brown sugar

1 tablespoon lemon juice

4 cloves

1/4 teaspoon ground mace

1/4 teaspoon ground nutmeg

1. Heat the tomatoes in a heavy pot over medium-low heat, and cook, stirring, until they start breaking down and come to a simmer.

2. Mix in the sugar, brown sugar, lemon juice, cloves, mace, and nutmeg, reduce the heat to low, and cook, occasionally stirring, until you have a jamlike paste, about 3 hours. Serve chilled as a jam or jelly and store in the refrigerator.

Relish is another one of those condiments that we should all try homemade at least once in our lives.

Ripe Tomato Relish

Makes 2 cups

1/2 cup cider vinegar

1/2 cup brown sugar

1/2 teaspoon pickling spice

1/2 teaspoon salt

1/2 teaspoon freshly ground
    black pepper

2 cups chopped fresh tomatoes

1/4 cup chopped celery

1/2 cup chopped yellow
    bell pepper

1/2 cup chopped onion

1 small hot pepper, chopped

1. Heat the vinegar, sugar, pickling spice, salt, and ground pepper in a saucepan over medium heat. Cook, stirring, until all the sugar and salt have dissolved and the mixture comes to a simmer, about 5 minutes.

2. Add the tomatoes, celery, bell pepper, onion, and hot pepper, and simmer, occasionally stirring, uncovered over medium-low heat until all the vegetables are tender and much of the liquid they've released has evaporated, about 1 hour. You'll know the relish is ready when the cooking liquid returns to a syrupy consistency.

3. Remove from the heat and transfer to a nonmetallic container. Plastic or glass both work fine here. Store in the refrigerator.

The Tomato Growers: Culton Organics

When I heard that Tom Culton's farm, Culton Organics, was located right outside Lancaster, Pennsylvania, I thought I knew what I'd be in for. After all, the place has a history and tradition of farming that goes back hundreds of years and has seen a steady flow of tourists for almost as long. So when Tom Culton appeared at his front door, looking for all the world like an alternative-rock megastar, I wanted to take a few minutes to get my bearings.

Did he give me a chance? Nope, not at all. Before I could get my laptop out, he was telling me how the farm has been in his family for seventy-seven years, that he viewed current organic regulations as inadequate, and how hard it was to find any trace of the old Pennsylvania Dutch culture anymore. Soon after that, he was sprinting through his fields and expecting me to keep up.

At the ripe old age of twenty-six, Tom has managed to inherit a marginal farm and turn it into an organic powerhouse. This isn't as easy as it sounds. Despite Lancaster's reputation as home of the wholesome Amish, "organic" is viewed here as the farming method of back-to-the-land city folk—something Tom certainly isn't. He knows the score, though, and said, "That's the way of farming; if you're not out in the forefront, you're struggling in the back. You've got to produce a premium product and put it on the plates of the best restaurants."

Tom is a classic example of what some people call the "Beyond Organic" movement. For example, he doesn't use manures because they might harbor disease. He then spelled out his ideas at a speed normally associated with jet aircraft. "We don't overthink. We're not chemists; that confuses things in farming. From seed to harvest, I am the responsible party." He continued, "I want to be as far away from GMOs [genetically modified organisms] as I can." His produce isn't certified organic because he insists Pennsylvania is too lax. Expressing rage at the idea that food can be both organic and imported from another continent, he declared, "I don't fertilize and I don't irrigate."

Tom grew up on Pennsylvania Dutch cooking, with dishes like stuffed pig stomach and canned sides gracing his family's table. Today, though, the food he wants to eat is "the freshest—something I can pick out and put on my plate in 20 minutes. Now I like a lot of raw food, I like raw salads. When I can feel instant energy from the foods I eat, that means it just tastes good." His favorite ways to eat tomatoes? Gazpacho or deep-fried green.

Tom told me, "I value every minute I have on this farm here. Farming for me is a liberating experience. I've worked regular jobs before. Farming frees me."

Chutneys began as the Indian version of relishes, but these days, the word can mean something that's authentically Indian or something that just has a few Asian spices. Chutney is meant to be served as a condiment with Indian food, but it can go almost anywhere hot sauce or relish would.

 ## Tomato Chutney
Makes 2 cups

2 tablespoons peanut oil

1 teaspoon mustard powder

1/4 teaspoon asafoetida (called *hing* in Indian grocery stores)

2 teaspoons ground coriander

1/4 cup finely chopped garlic cloves

2 tablespoons finely chopped fresh ginger

2 tablespoons finely chopped fresh hot chili pepper

3 cups chopped fresh tomatoes

1/2 cup cider vinegar

2 tablespoons sugar

1 teaspoon salt

1. Heat the oil, mustard powder, asafoetida, and coriander in a pot over medium heat, and cook, stirring, until the spices are evenly coated with oil and the mixture begins to bubble, about 30 seconds.

2. Mix in the garlic, ginger, and chili, cooking until the garlic becomes tender, about 5 minutes.

3. Add the tomatoes, vinegar, sugar, and salt, and return the mixture to a simmer. Reduce the heat to low and continue to cook, occasionally stirring, until the mixture becomes a thick paste, about 30 minutes.

A few years ago it was announced that, somehow, salsa had overtaken ketchup as America's number-one condiment. This was apparently a revolutionary event. Of course, as is so often the case, I didn't get it. People didn't dip chips in ketchup, and while both wound up on eggs every now and then, it seemed like you needed much more salsa for one serving than you did ketchup. Ketchup and salsa do have one thing in common though: Packaging kills most of the flavor. Make them both fresh and leave the jars and bottles behind.

I keep encountering salsa recipes with everything in them from mango to chocolate. We'll pass on that stuff and just serve up a classic.

Salsa
Makes 3 cups

2 cups chopped fresh
   tomatoes
1/2 teaspoon salt
2 cloves garlic, finely
   chopped
1/2 cup chopped red onion
1/2 cup chopped green
   bell pepper

4 small chili peppers,
   chopped
1/4 cup chopped
   coriander leaves
1/4 cup chopped Italian
   parsley
2 tablespoons freshly
   squeezed lime juice.

1. Put the tomatoes in a colander, sprinkle them with the salt, toss them, and let them drain for about 30 minutes.

2. In a large bowl, mix the drained tomatoes, garlic, onion, bell pepper, chili, coriander, parsley, and lime juice. Toss and make sure everything is well combined.

3. Refrigerate the mixture for at least 1 hour before serving to let the flavors combine. Store any extra in the refrigerator.

Are you curious? Tired of orange marmalade? Sick of grape jelly? Well, then, get ready for something different. . . .

 ## Tomato Marmalade

Makes 2 cups

4 cups chopped fresh
    plum tomatoes
1/2 cup chopped fresh
    orange with rind
1/4 cup chopped fresh lemon
    with rind
1/4 cup chopped fresh lime
    with rind
3 cinnamon sticks
1 tablespoon slivered
    fresh ginger
5 whole cloves
1/2 teaspoon whole allspice
1 cup sugar
1 cup brown sugar

1. Heat the tomatoes, orange, lemon, lime, cinnamon, ginger, cloves, and allspice in a heavy pot over low heat, and bring to a simmer. Mix in the sugar and brown sugar, and cook, stirring, until all the sugar is dissolved.

2. Continue cooking uncovered over low heat until the mixture takes on a thick and jamlike consistency. The marmalade is ready when it's the as thick as a typical jam, about 2 hours. Remove the cinnamon sticks, and pour the marmalade into a resealable container while still warm. Store in the refrigerator.

Fruit or Vegetable?

Generations of schoolchildren, botanists, and food fanatics have made a point of reminding me that tomatoes are fruits. They explain that they grow on vines and consist of seeds enclosed by delicious, edible stuff. (That might not exactly be a definition of "fruit," but it's the way I understand it.) When I point out that this means that cucumbers, peppers and maybe even snowpeas would be fruits, too, they just stare at me with the sort of look that says, "Read a book or two about botany, and call me in the morning."

It seems to me that the tomato's role in meat sauce, tomato rice soup, and curry would seal the vegetable argument—would you describe a Greek salad as a "fruit salad"? In fact, this is just what the Supreme Court said in the legendary legal case "Nix v. Hedden." Back in 1893, the Nixes were importing tomatoes and paying the high duties levied on vegetables. They felt they should have been charged the much lower rate set for fruit; after all, dictionaries say it's a fruit. The justices disagreed. They felt that because tomatoes are commonly used as vegetables, they should be taxed as vegetables. Yes, a vegetable.

I rest my case. . . .

I know that in places like Kansas City or North Carolina, people fight over barbecue sauce recipes all the time. I wasn't looking for an argument, just something that wasn't bottled, canned, or sitting on the shelf for six months.

Use this barbecue sauce both for cooking and on the table as a condiment. Sometimes I like it instead of ketchup or mustard.

 ## Barbecue Sauce
Makes 1 pint

1 tablespoon peanut oil
1/2 teaspoon paprika
1 teaspoon crushed
    chili flakes
1/4 teaspoon
    ground cloves
1/2 teaspoon dry
    mustard
2 cups chopped onions
2 cups canned
    crushed tomatoes or
    passata (page 20)

2 canned chipotle
    peppers, chopped,
    plus 1 teaspoon
    sauce from
    the can
1/2 cup cider vinegar
1/4 cup molasses
2 tablespoons
    brown sugar
1/2 teaspoon salt
1/2 teaspoon freshly
    ground black pepper

1. Heat the oil, paprika, chili flakes, cloves, and mustard in a heavy pot over medium heat. Cook, stirring, until the spices are coated with oil, about 1 minute.

2. Reduce the heat to low, and add the onions. Cook, occasionally stirring, until the onions are very tender and have absorbed all the spice flavoring, about 60 minutes.

3. Add the tomatoes, chipotle peppers and sauce, vinegar, molasses, brown sugar, salt, and ground pepper, and simmer uncovered with occasional stirring until the onions have dissolved, the tomatoes have broken down, and one-quarter of the liquid has evaporated, about 60 minutes. Remove from the heat.

4. Purée the mixture in a blender, transfer it to a recloseable container, and store in the refrigerator.

Like salsa, "train smash" can be either a sauce or a condiment. Indeed, I have it on good authority that in South Africa—where it also carries the name "braai relish"—it's most commonly bought as a prepared product. The rest of us will have to make it ourselves.

South Africans serve train smash as a sauce with all sorts of things, including the usual items like grilled meats and something they call "pap." American cooks will instantly recognize pap as polenta. Indeed, you can head over to your local Italian grocery and buy the fixings for an authentic South African meal.

South African Train Smash

Makes 3 cups

1 tablespoon peanut oil

2 cups chopped onions

3 cups canned crushed tomatoes or *passata* (page 20)

1/4 cup white vinegar

2 tablespoons Worcestershire sauce

2 tablespoons sugar

1/2 teaspoon dry mustard powder

1/2 teaspoon salt

1/2 teaspoon freshly ground black pepper

1. Heat the oil and onions in a saucepan over medium heat and cook, stirring, until the onions are translucent and tender, about 20 minutes.

2. Add the tomatoes and simmer, occasionally stirring, until the raw tomato taste is gone, about 20 minutes.

3. Mix in the vinegar, Worcestershire, sugar, mustard powder, salt, and ground pepper, cooking, occasionally stirring, until the flavors are combined and the volume is reduced by about one-third, about 45 minutes. Your train smash should be about the same thickness as a relish. Let cool, and store in the refrigerator.

Everybody seems to be into making hot sauce these days, and fancy shops are filled with creatively named products. Isn't it time you started making your own, too? And I suggest that instead of calling your finished sauce "Tomato Chipotle Habanero Hot Sauce," you come up with the sort of colorful name that artisan sauce bottlers love.

You'll need rubber gloves for handling the peppers.

Tomato Chipotle Habanero Hot Sauce
Makes 1 cup

1 tablespoon olive oil
1 teaspoon ground
    cumin
1/2 teaspoon salt
1/2 teaspoon freshly
    ground black
    pepper
4 canned chipotle
    peppers plus 1
    tablespoon sauce
    from the can

1 habanero pepper,
    finely chopped*
1 cup canned crushed
    tomato or *passata*
    (page 20)
1 tablespoon brown
    sugar
1 cup cider vinegar
*Not hot enough for
you? Add a second
habanero.

1. Heat the oil, cumin, salt, and ground pepper in a saucepan over medium heat. Cook, stirring, until the oil coats the spices, about 1 minute.

2. Mix in the chipotle peppers and sauce and the habanero. Cook until the habanero becomes tender, about 15 minutes. Remember to handle the habanero with gloves and *do not* taste-test the mixture just yet.

3. Add the tomatoes, sugar, and vinegar, and reduce the heat to medium-low. Simmer until half the liquid has evaporated, about 1 hour. Remove from the heat and let cool.

4. Purée the mixture in a food processor. Store in a tightly capped container in the refrigerator.

10. desserts

There are times when you want a written recipe because a dish has so many ingredients that you need notes to keep track of them all and times when a dish is assembled in a complex or unusual way. But Korean-Style Tomatoes Sprinkled with Sugar isn't either of these. Instead, it needs to be written down just so you know that by sprinkling a bit of sugar on a sliced tomato, you can turn it into a dessert.

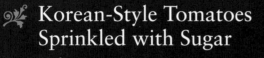

Korean-Style Tomatoes Sprinkled with Sugar

Makes 4 servings

2 large tomatoes, halved
3 tablespoons sugar or vanilla sugar

1. Lay the tomato halves on serving plates, cut side up.

2. Sprinkle the sugar on the tomatoes. Serve immediately.

While I'm certainly not the sort of person who frequents Parisian three-star restaurants, I am well aware that one of the most famous, Arpège, serves a tomato dessert. Needless to say, recreating a three-star dish is no easy task, but this simple version gives you a clear idea of how tomato can be the basis of an amazing dessert.

 ## Roasted Tomatoes with Twelve Flavors

Makes 4 Servings

1 tablespoon butter plus extra for baking dish

1/2 cup chopped fresh pear

1/2 cup chopped fresh apple

1/2 cup chopped fresh pineapple

1 cup orange juice

1/4 cup chopped walnuts

1/4 cup chopped almonds

1/4 cup shelled pistachios

1/4 cup raisins

1 teaspoon orange zest

1 teaspoon lemon zest

1 tablespoon chopped fresh mint leaves

1 teaspoon vanilla extract

4 cloves

1/2 cup sugar

4 medium tomatoes

1. Preheat the oven to 375 degrees.

2. Heat the butter, pear, apple, pineapple, orange juice, walnuts, almonds, pistachios, raisins, orange zest, lemon zest, mint, vanilla extract, cloves, and sugar in a saucepan over medium low heat. Cook, stirring, until all the fruits are tender and a syrup has formed, about 20 minutes. Keep warm until you're ready for step 4.

3. Make sure your tomatoes can stand up on their own. If they can't, slice a bit off the bottom. Now use a melon baller or grapefruit spoon to hollow out the insides. Place the hollowed-out tomatoes on a buttered baking dish.

4. Stuff the hollowed-out tomatoes with the fruit mixture. Pour any remaining liquid over the tomatoes.

5. Bake until all the fruit is cooked through, about 40 minutes. Serve warm.

Tomato Soup Cake is one of those recipes that every baking fan has heard of but few have tried. Undoubtedly some of you are crying out, "How could this be edible?!" or maybe just, "Give me a break!" You'll see. . . .

Tomato Soup Cake

Makes 1 cake, about 8 servings

1/2 cup shortening
1/2 cup white sugar
1/2 cup brown sugar
1 can (10 3/4 ounces)
    condensed tomato soup
1 teaspoon baking soda
2 cups flour
1 teaspoon ground cinnamon
1/2 teaspoon ground allspice
1/2 teaspoon ground nutmeg
1/2 teaspoon ground cloves
1/2 cup raisins
1/2 cup crushed or
    chopped pecans
Oil for baking pan

1. Preheat the oven to 325 degrees.

2. Cream the shortening and sugars together in a large bowl.

3. Add the soup to the shortening and sugar and mix well.

4. Sift the baking soda and flour together and fold into the soup mixture. It should form a thick batter. If it's too dry, add water 1/4 cup at a time until it's just a bit thicker than pancake batter.

5. Add the cinnamon, allspice, nutmeg, cloves, raisins, and pecans, making sure that all the ingredients are evenly distributed.

6. Pour the mixture into a well-oiled loaf pan and bake for 60 minutes or until a toothpick inserted into the top comes out dry. Let cool for 10 minutes before serving.

Down in southern New Jersey, where tomatoes dominate cuisine and culture, there just had to be a tomato dessert. Despite denials by the locals, recipes like this one turned up with just a bit of research.

Green Tomato Pie
Makes 1 pie

3 cups chopped green tomatoes

2 cups chopped Granny Smith
    or similar baking apples

1/2 cup sugar

1 cup brown sugar

1 cup raisins

1 teaspoon ground cinnamon

1/2 teaspoon ground cloves

1/2 teaspoon ground allspice

2 tablespoons lemon juice

1 two-layer piecrust dough

1. Preheat the oven to 375 degrees.

2. Combine the tomatoes, apples, sugar, brown sugar, raisins, cinnamon, cloves, allspice, and lemon juice in a large bowl, and toss until all the ingredients are evenly distributed.

2. Line a pie pan with the bottom piecrust dough and pour in the tomato mixture. Cover with the top layer of dough, seal the edges, and poke a few holes in the top so that steam can escape.

3. Bake for 1 hour or until the edges of the crust are deeply browned. Let cool for at least 15 minutes before serving.

Index

Note: Page numbers in *italics* refer to photographs